The comical revenge, or, Love in a tub as it is now acted at Her Majesty's theatre / by Sir George Etherege. (1689)

George Etherege

Early English Books Online (EEBO) Editions

Imagine holding history in your hands.

Now you can. Digitally preserved and previously accessible only through libraries as Early English Books Online, this rare material is now available in single print editions. Thousands of books written between 1475 and 1700 and ranging from religion to astronomy, medicine to music, can be delivered to your doorstep in individual volumes of high-quality historical reproductions.

We have been compiling these historic treasures for more than 70 years. Long before such a thing as "digital" even existed, ProQuest founder Eugene Power began the noble task of preserving the British Museum's collection on microfilm. He then sought out other rare and endangered titles, providing unparalleled access to these works and collaborating with the world's top academic institutions to make them widely available for the first time. This project furthers that original vision.

These texts have now made the full journey -- from their original printing-press versions available only in rare-book rooms to online library access to new single volumes made possible by the partnership between artifact preservation and modern printing technology. A portion of the proceeds from every book sold supports the libraries and institutions that made this collection possible, and that still work to preserve these invaluable treasures passed down through time.

This is history, traveling through time since the dawn of printing to your own personal library.

Initial Proquest EEBO Print Editions collections include:

Early Literature

This comprehensive collection begins with the famous Elizabethan Era that saw such literary giants as Chaucer, Shakespeare and Marlowe, as well as the introduction of the sonnet. Traveling through Jacobean and Restoration literature, the highlight of this series is the Pollard and Redgrave 1475-1640 selection of the rarest works from the English Renaissance.

Early Documents of World History

This collection combines early English perspectives on world history with documentation of Parliament records, royal decrees and military documents that reveal the delicate balance of Church and State in early English government. For social historians, almanacs and calendars offer insight into daily life of common citizens. This exhaustively complete series presents a thorough picture of history through the English Civil War.

Historical Almanacs

Historically, almanacs served a variety of purposes from the more practical, such as planting and harvesting crops and plotting nautical routes, to predicting the future through the movements of the stars. This collection provides a wide range of consecutive years of "almanacks" and calendars that depict a vast array of everyday life as it was several hundred years ago.

Early History of Astronomy & Space

Humankind has studied the skies for centuries, seeking to find our place in the universe. Some of the most important discoveries in the field of astronomy were made in these texts recorded by ancient stargazers, but almost as impactful were the perspectives of those who considered their discoveries to be heresy. Any independent astronomer will find this an invaluable collection of titles arguing the truth of the cosmic system.

Early History of Industry & Science

Acting as a kind of historical Wall Street, this collection of industry manuals and records explores the thriving industries of construction; textile, especially wool and linen; salt; livestock; and many more.

Early English Wit, Poetry & Satire

The power of literary device was never more in its prime than during this period of history, where a wide array of political and religious satire mocked the status quo and poetry called humankind to transcend the rigors of daily life through love, God or principle. This series comments on historical patterns of the human condition that are still visible today.

Early English Drama & Theatre

This collection needs no introduction, combining the works of some of the greatest canonical writers of all time, including many plays composed for royalty such as Queen Elizabeth I and King Edward VI. In addition, this series includes history and criticism of drama, as well as examinations of technique.

Early History of Travel & Geography

Offering a fascinating view into the perception of the world during the sixteenth and seventeenth centuries, this collection includes accounts of Columbus's discovery of the Americas and encompasses most of the Age of Discovery, during which Europeans and their descendants intensively explored and mapped the world. This series is a wealth of information from some the most groundbreaking explorers.

Early Fables & Fairy Tales

This series includes many translations, some illustrated, of some of the most well-known mythologies of today, including Aesop's Fables and English fairy tales, as well as many Greek, Latin and even Oriental parables and criticism and interpretation on the subject.

Early Documents of Language & Linguistics

The evolution of English and foreign languages is documented in these original texts studying and recording early philology from the study of a variety of languages including Greek, Latin and Chinese, as well as multilingual volumes, to current slang and obscure words. Translations from Latin, Hebrew and Aramaic, grammar treatises and even dictionaries and guides to translation make this collection rich in cultures from around the world.

Early History of the Law

With extensive collections of land tenure and business law "forms" in Great Britain, this is a comprehensive resource for all kinds of early English legal precedents from feudal to constitutional law, Jewish and Jesuit law, laws about public finance to food supply and forestry, and even "immoral conditions." An abundance of law dictionaries, philosophy and history and criticism completes this series.

Early History of Kings, Queens and Royalty

This collection includes debates on the divine right of kings, royal statutes and proclamations, and political ballads and songs as related to a number of English kings and queens, with notable concentrations on foreign rulers King Louis IX and King Louis XIV of France, and King Philip II of Spain. Writings on ancient rulers and royal tradition focus on Scottish and Roman kings, Cleopatra and the Biblical kings Nebuchadnezzar and Solomon.

Early History of Love, Marriage & Sex

Human relationships intrigued and baffled thinkers and writers well before the postmodern age of psychology and self-help. Now readers can access the insights and intricacies of Anglo-Saxon interactions in sex and love, marriage and politics, and the truth that lies somewhere in between action and thought.

Early History of Medicine, Health & Disease

This series includes fascinating studies on the human brain from as early as the 16th century, as well as early studies on the physiological effects of tobacco use. Anatomy texts, medical treatises and wound treatment are also discussed, revealing the exponential development of medical theory and practice over more than two hundred years.

Early History of Logic, Science and Math

The "hard sciences" developed exponentially during the 16th and 17th centuries, both relying upon centuries of tradition and adding to the foundation of modern application, as is evidenced by this extensive collection. This is a rich collection of practical mathematics as applied to business, carpentry and geography as well as explorations of mathematical instruments and arithmetic; logic and logicians such as Aristotle and Socrates; and a number of scientific disciplines from natural history to physics.

Early History of Military, War and Weaponry

Any professional or amateur student of war will thrill at the untold riches in this collection of war theory and practice in the early Western World. The Age of Discovery and Enlightenment was also a time of great political and religious unrest, revealed in accounts of conflicts such as the Wars of the Roses.

Early History of Food

This collection combines the commercial aspects of food handling, preservation and supply to the more specific aspects of canning and preserving, meat carving, brewing beer and even candy-making with fruits and flowers, with a large resource of cookery and recipe books. Not to be forgotten is a "the great eater of Kent," a study in food habits.

Early History of Religion

From the beginning of recorded history we have looked to the heavens for inspiration and guidance. In these early religious documents, sermons, and pamphlets, we see the spiritual impact on the lives of both royalty and the commoner. We also get insights into a clergy that was growing ever more powerful as a political force. This is one of the world's largest collections of religious works of this type, revealing much about our interpretation of the modern church and spirituality.

Early Social Customs

Social customs, human interaction and leisure are the driving force of any culture. These unique and quirky works give us a glimpse of interesting aspects of day-to-day life as it existed in an earlier time. With books on games, sports, traditions, festivals, and hobbies it is one of the most fascinating collections in the series.

The BiblioLife Network

This project was made possible in part by the BiblioLife Network (BLN), a project aimed at addressing some of the huge challenges facing book preservationists around the world. The BLN includes libraries, library networks, archives, subject matter experts, online communities and library service providers. We believe every book ever published should be available as a high-quality print reproduction; printed on-demand anywhere in the world. This insures the ongoing accessibility of the content and helps generate sustainable revenue for the libraries and organizations that work to preserve these important materials.

The following book is in the "public domain" and represents an authentic reproduction of the text as printed by the original publisher. While we have attempted to accurately maintain the integrity of the original work, there are sometimes problems with the original work or the micro-film from which the books were digitized. This can result in minor errors in reproduction. Possible imperfections include missing and blurred pages, poor pictures, markings and other reproduction issues beyond our control. Because this work is culturally important, we have made it available as part of our commitment to protecting, preserving, and promoting the world's literature.

GUIDE TO FOLD-OUTS MAPS and OVERSIZED IMAGES

The book you are reading was digitized from microfilm captured over the past thirty to forty years. Years after the creation of the original microfilm, the book was converted to digital files and made available in an online database.

In an online database, page images do not need to conform to the size restrictions found in a printed book. When converting these images back into a printed bound book, the page sizes are standardized in ways that maintain the detail of the original. For large images, such as fold-out maps, the original page image is split into two or more pages

Guidelines used to determine how to split the page image follows:

• Some images are split vertically; large images require vertical and horizontal splits.
• For horizontal splits, the content is split left to right.
• For vertical splits, the content is split from top to bottom.
• For both vertical and horizontal splits, the image is processed from top left to bottom right.

THE
Comical Revenge;

OR,

LOVE
IN A
TUB.

As it is now Acted

At Her Majesty's Theatre.

By Sir *George Etherege*.

LONDON,

Printed for *H. Herringman,* and are to be sold by *Francis Saunders*
at the *Blue Anchor,* in the Lower Walk of the
New-Exchange, 1 6 8 9.

TO THE

Right Honourable

CHARLES

EARL of

DORSET and MIDDLESEX,

Lord Chamberlain of his Majesty's Houshold,
Lord Lieutenant of *Suffex*, and one of their
Majesties most Honourable Privy-Council.

My Lord,

I Cou'd not have wish'd my self more fortunate than I have been in the success of this
Poem. The Writing of it was a means to
make me known to your Lordship; The Acting
of it has lost me no Reputation; And the Printing of it has now given me an Opportunity to
shew how much I honour you.

I here dedicate it, as I have long since dedi-

cated

cated my self, to your Lordſhip: Let the humble Love of the Giver make you ſet ſome value
upon the worthleſs Gift: I hope it may have
ſome eſteem with others, becauſe the Author
knows how to eſteem you, whoſe Knowledge
moves admiration, and Goodneſs love, in all
that know you. But I deſign this a Dedication,
not a Panegyrick; not to proclaim your Virtues
to the World, but to ſhew your Lordſhip how
firmly they have oblig'd me to be,

My Lord,

Your moſt humble

and Faithful Servant,

GEO. ETHEREGE.

Per-

Perſonæ Dramatis.

THE Lord Bevil,   Father to *Lovis, Graciana* and *Aurelia*.
The Lord Beaufort,   Servant to *Graciana*.
Colonel Bruce,   A Cavalier, Friend to *Lovis*, in love with *Graciana*.
Lovis,   Friend to *Bruce*.
Sir Frederick Frollick,   Couſin to the Lord *Beaufort*.
Graciana,   A young Lady, in love with the Lord *Beaufort*.
Aurelia,   Her Siſter in love with Col. *Bruce*.
Mrs. Rich,   A wealthy Widow, Siſter to the Lord *Bevill*, in love with Sir *Frederick*.
Leticia,   A Girl, waiting upon *Aurelia*.
Betty,   Waiting-woman to the Widow.
Dufoy,   A ſaucy impertinent French-man, Servant to Sir *Frederick*.
Clark,   Servant to the Lord *Beaufort*.
Sir Nicholas Cully,   Knighted by *Oliver*.
Wheadle
  and   }   Gameſters.
Palmer,
Mrs. Grace,   A Wench kept by *Wheadle*.
Jenny,   Her Maid.
Mrs. Lucy.   A Wench kept by Sir *Frederick*.
A Coach-man belonging to the Widow.
A Bell-man.
Foot-men, Link-boys, Drawers, and other Attendants.

THE

THE
PROLOGUE.

WHO cou'd expect such crowding here to day,
Meerly on the report of a new Play?
A Man wou'd think y' ave been so often bit
By us of late, you shou'd have learn'd more wit,
And first have sent a Forlorn Hope to spy
The Plot and Language of our Comedy,
Expecting till some desp'rate Criticks had
Resolv'd you whether it were good or bad:
But yet we hope you'l never grow so wife;
For if you shou'd, we and our Comedies
Must trip to Norwich, or for Ireland go,
And never fix; but, like a Puppet-show,
Remove from Town to Town, from Fair to Fair,
Seeking fit Chapmen to put off our Ware.
For such our Fortune is this barren Age,
That Faction now, not Wit, supports the Stage:
Wit has, like Painting, had her happy flights,
And in peculiar Ages reach'd her heights,
Though now declin'd; yet cou'd some able Pen
Match Fletcher's Nature, or the Art of Ben,
The Old and Graver sort wou'd scarce allow
Those Plays were good, because we writ them now.
Our Author therefore begs you wou'd forget,
Most Reverend Judges, the Records of Wit,
And only think upon the modern way
Of writing, whilst y' are censuring his Play.
And Gallants, as for you, talk loud i' th' Pit,
Divert your selves and Friends with your own Wit;
Observe the Ladies, and neglect the Play,
Or else 'tis fear'd we are undone to day.

THE

THE
Comical Revenge;
OR,
LOVE in a TUB.

ACT I. SCENE I.

The Scene, An Anti-Chamber to Sir *Frederick*
Frolick's Bed-Chamber.

Enter Dufoy, *with a Plaifter on his head, walking difcontentedly;*
and Clark *immediately after him.*

Clark. **G**Ood-morrow, *Monfieur.*
   Dufoy. Good-mor', ——— Good mor'.
   Clark. Is Sir *Fred'rick* ftirring?
   Dufoy. Pox fturré himé.
   Clark. My Lord has fent me ———
   Dufoy. Begar me vil havé de revengé; me vil no
Stay two day in *Englandé.*
   Clark. Good *Monfieur*, what's the matter?
   Dufoy. De matré! de matré is eafie to be perceive;
Dis Bedlamé, Mad-capé, diable de matré, vas
Drunké de laft night; and vor no reafon, but dat
Me did advifé him to go to Bed, Begar he did

                               Striké

Striké, breaké my headé, Jernie.

 Clark. Have patience, he did it unadvisedly.

 Dufoy. Unadvisé! didé not me advise him

Justé when he did ité?

 Clark. Yes; but he was in drink you say.

 Duf. In drinké; me vishé he had been over de head

And de ear in drinké; Begar in *France* de

Drink dat van Man drinké does not crack de

Noder Mans brainé. Hark!   [*Sir Fred: knocks.*

He is avaké, and none of the people are

To attendé himé: Ian Villian day are all gone, run. [*Knocks again.*

To the Diable; have de patience, I beseech you.

       [*Pointing towards his Master's Chamber*]

 Clark. Acquaint Sir *Frederick*, I am here from my Lord.

 Duf. I vil, I vil; your venumble Serviteur. [*Exeunt.*

SCENE II.

Scene, Sir *Frederick*'s Bed-Chamber.

Enter Sir Frederick *in his night-gown, and after him* Dufoy.

 Dufoy. Good mor', good-mor, to your Vorshippé; me am alvay

Ready to attendé you Vorshippé, and your Vorshippé's

Alvay ready to beaté and to abuse mé; you vare drunké

De lasté nighté, and my head aké to day morningé;

Seé you here if my brainé have no ver good raison [*Shewing his head.*

To counsel you, and to mindé your bus'nessé.

 Sir Fred. Thou hast a notable brain;

Set me down a Crown for a

Plaister; but forbear your rebukes.

 Duf. 'Tis ver couragious sting to breaké de head of your

Serviteur, is it noté? Begar you vil never keepé

De good Serviteur, had no me love you ver vel. ——

 Sir Fred. I know thou lov'st me.

 Duf. And darefore you do beaté me, is dat de raison?

 Sir Fred. Prethee forbear, I am sorry for't.

 Duf. Ver good satisfaction! Begar it is me dat am sorrié for't.

 Sir Fred. Well, well.

 Duf. De Serviteur of my Lord your Cousin

Be comé speak vid you,

 Sir Fred. Bring him in.   [*Exit Dufoy.*

I am of opinion that drunkenness is not so

Damnable a sin to me as 'tis to many; Sorrow

          And

And Repentance are fure to be my firſt Work
The next Morning: 'slid, I have known fome
So lucky at this Recreation, that, whereas 'tis
Familiar to forget what we do in drink,
Have even loſt the memory after Sleep, of being drunk:
Now do I feel more Qualms,
Than a young Woman in Breeding.

        Enter Dufoy *and* Clark.   [Dufoy *goes out again.*

Clark! What News from the God of Love?
He's always at your Maſter's Elbow;
H'as joſtl'd the Devil out of Service; no more!
Mrs. *Grace!* Poor Girl, Mrs. *Graciana* has flung
A Squibb into his Boſome, where the Wild fire will
Huzzéé for a time, and then crack,
It flies out at's Breeches.

    Clark. Sir, he ſent me before with his Service;
He'll wait on you himſelf when he's dreſs'd.

    Sir Fred. In very good time;
There never was a Girl more humourſome.
Nor tedious in the Dreſſing of her Baby.   [*Ex.* Clark.

        Enter Dufoy, *and* Foot-Boy.

    Dufoy. Hayé! Heré is de ver fine varké,
Begar, de ver vine Varké!———

    Sir Fred. What's the Buſineſs?

    Dufoy. De Buſineſs! De Divel také mé if dare be not
De whole Regiment Army de Hackené Cocheman,
De Link-Boy, de Fydler, and de Shamber Mayde,
Dat havé beſeegé de Howsé; dis is de conſequance
Of de Drink, vid a Poxé.

    Sir Fred. Well, The Coach-men and Link-boys muſt be
Satisfy'd, I ſuppoſe there's Money due to 'em;
The Fidlers, for broken Heads and Inſtruments,
Muſt be compounded with; I leave that to your Care:
But for the Chamber-maid, I'll deal with her my ſelf;
Go, go, fetch her up.

    Dufoy. De Pimpé, begar, I vil be de Pimpé to no Man
In de Chriſtendomé; do you go fetch her up;
De Pimpé———
                           [*Ex.* Dufoy.

    Sir Fred. Go, Sirrah, direct her.   [*to the* Foot-boy.]   [*Ex.* Foot-boy.
Now have I moſt unmanfully fallen foul upon ſome
Woman, I'll warrant you, and wounded her
Reputation ſhrowardly: Oh Drink, Drink!
Thou art a vile Enemy to the civilleſt ſort of
Courteous Ladies.———

                         B

Enter Jenny, *Wheadle's Wanch's Maid.*

Oh *Jenny*, next my Heart nothing could
Be more welcome.

Maid. Unhand me;
Are you a Man fit to be trusted with a Woman's
Reputation?

Sir Fred. Not when I am in a reeling Condition;
Men are now and then subject to those Infirmities
In Drink, which Women have when they are sober.
Drunkenness is no good Secretary, *Jenny*;
You must not look so angry, good Faith, you must not.

Maid. Angry! We always took you for a civil Gentleman.

Sir Fred. So I am, i' troth, I think.———

Maid. A civil Gentleman will
Come to a Ladies Lodging at two a Clock
In the Morning, and knock as if it were upon
Life and Death; a Midwife never was knock'd up
With more Fury!

Sir Fred. Well, well, Girl, All's well, I hope, all's well.

Maid. You have made such an Uproar amongst
Our Neighbours, we must be forc'd to change
Our Lodging.

Sir Fred. And thou art come to tell me whither———
Kind Heart!

Maid. I'll see you a little better manner'd first.
Because we would not let you in at that unseasonable Hour,
You, and your rude ranting Companions
Hoop'd and hollow'd like Mad-men,
And roar'd out in the Streets,
A Whore, A Whore, A Whore; you need not
Have knock'd good People out of their Beds,
You might have met with them had been
Good enough for your Purpose abroad.

Sir Fred. 'Twas ill done, *Jenny*, indeed it was.

Maid. 'Twas a Mercy, Mr. *Wheadle* was not there,
My Mistresses Friend; had he been there sh'ad been quite undone.
There's nothing got by your lewd Doings: you are
But Scandals to a civil Woman: We had so much
The good Will of the Neighbours before, we had
Credit for what we wou'd; and but this Morning
The Chandler refus'd to score a Quart of Scurvey-grass.

Sir Fred. Hang Reputation among a Company of Rascals;
Trust me not, if thou art not grown most wondrous pretty. [*Offers to hug her.*

Maid. Stand off, or I protest I'll make the People.

In

In your Lodging to know what manner of
Man you are.

Sir Fred. You and I have been intimate Acquaintance; ———
why so coy now, *Jenny?*

Maid. 'Pray forbear: ———
You'l never leave till I shriek out; ———Your   *[Noise within.*
Servants listen, hark ———there's some body coming.
My Mistress charg'd me to tell you, she will   *[Enter* Beafort.
Never see your Eyes again; she never deserv'd
This at your hands, ———poor Gentlewoman! ——— You had a
Fling at me too, you did not whisper it, I thank you:
'Tis a miserable Condition we
Women bring our selves to for your sakes.   *[Weeps.*

Beauf. How now Cosin? what, at wars with the Women?

Sir Fred. I gave a small alarm to their Quarters
Last night, my Lord.

Beauf. Jenny in tears! what's the Occasion, poor Girl?

Maid. I'll tell you, my Lord.

Sir Fred. Buzze; Set not her tongue a going agen;
    [Clapping his hand before her Mouth.
Sh'as made more noise than half a dozen Paper-mills:
London-bridge at a low water is silence to her;
In a word, rambling last night,
We knockt at her Mistresses Lodging,
They deny'd us entrance, whereupon,
A harsh word or two flew out, *Whore*——. I think,
Or something to that purpose.

Maid. These were not all your Heroick Actions;   *[Enter* Dufoy.
Pray tell the Consequence, how you march'd bravely
At the Rear of an Army of Link-boys;
Upon the sudden, how you gave defiance,
And then wag'd a bloody War with the Constable;
And having vanquisht that dreadful Enemy,
How you committed a general Massacre,
On the Glass-Windows: Are not these
Most honourable Atchievements, such as will be regiftred,
To your eternal Fame, by the most learn'd
Historians of *Hicks's-Hall.*

Sir Fred. Good sweet *Jenny,* let's come to a Treaty;
Do but hear what Articles I'll propose.

Maid. A Woman's Heart's too tender to be an Enemy
To Peace.   *[They whisper.*

Dufoy. Your most humble Serviteur, my Lord.

Beauf. Monsieur, I perceive you are much to blame;

    You

You are an excellent Governour indeed.

Dufoy. Begar do you tinké dat 1 amé de Bedlamé?
Notingé but Bedlame can governé himé.

Sir Fred. Jenny, here's my hand; I'll come,
And make amends for all —— pretty Rogue. ——

Dufoy. Ver pret Rogucé,
Vid a poxé.

Maid. What rude French Rafcal have you here?

Dufoy. Rafcalé! Begar ver it nod vor de reverence of my Matré,
I vod cut off your Occupation. French Rafcalé!
Whore Englifh ——

Sir Fred. Dufoy, be gone and leave us.

Dufoy. I vil, I vil leave you to your Recreation;
I vifh you ver good Paftimé, and de Poxé,
Begar.   [*Exit* Dufoy.

Maid. I never heard a ruder Fellow.—— Sir *Frederick,*
You will not fail the time.

Sir Fred, No, no, *Jenny.*

Maid. Your Servant, my Lord.

Beauf. Farewel, *Jenny.*   [*Exit* Jenny.

Sir Fred. Now did all this Fury end in a mild
Invitation to the Ladies Lodging.

Beauf. I have known this Wenches Miftrefs,
Ever fince I came from Travel,
But never was acquainted with that Fellow that keeps her;
Prithee, what is he?

Sir Fred. Why his name is *Wheadle*; he's one whofe trade is Treachery,
To make a Friend and then deceive him;
He's of a ready Wit, pleafant Converfation,
Throughly skill'd in Men; In a word,
He knows fo much of Virtue, as makes him
Well accomplifh'd for all manner of Vice:
He has lately infinuated himfelf into,
Sir *Nich'las Culley,* one whom *Oliver,*
For the tranfcendent Knavery and Difloyalty
Of his Father, has difhonour'd with Knight-hood;
A Fellow, as poor in Experience, as in Parts,
And one that has a vain-glorious Humour,
To gain a Reputation amongft the Gentry, by feigning good nature,
And an affection to the King, and his Party.
I made a little debauch, th'other day, in their Company,
Where I forefaw this Fellows Deftiny, his Purfe muft pay for
Keeping this Wench, and all other *Wheadle's* Extravagances.
But pray, my Lord,

                                                        How

How thrive you in your more honourable Adventures?
Is Harveſt near? When is the Sickle
To be put i'th'Corn?

Beauf. I have been hitherto ſo proſperous,
My Happineſs has ſtill out-flown my Faith:
Nothing remains but Ceremonial Charms,
Graciana's fix'd i'th' Circle of my Arms.

Sir Fred. Then y'are a happy Man for a ſeaſon.

Beauf. For ever.

Sir Fred. I miſtruſt your Miſtreſſes Divinity;
You'll find her Attributes but Mortal:
Women, like Juglers Tricks,
Appear Miracles to the Ignorant; but in themſelves,
Th'are mere Cheats.

Beauf. Well, well, Couſin, I have engag'd that you, this day,
Shall be my Gueſt at my Lord *Bevil*'s Table;
Pray make me Maſter of my Promiſe once.

Sir Fred. 'Faith I have engag'd to dine with my dear *Lucy*,
Poor Girl, I have lately given her Occaſion
To ſuſpeſt my kindneſs; yet, for your ſake,
I'll venture to break my Word,
Upon condition you'll excuſe my Errours;
You know my Converſation
Has not been amongſt ceremonious
Ladies.

Beauf. All modeſt Freedom you will find allow'd;
Formality is baniſh'd thence.

Sir Fred. This Virtue is enough to make me bear
With all the Inconveniencies of honeſt Company.

Beauf. The freeneſs of your Humour is your Friend.
I have ſuch news to tell thee, that, I fear,
Thou'lt find thy Breaſt too narrow for thy Joy.

Sir Fred. Gently, my Lord, leſt I find the thing too
Little for my Expeſtation.

Beauf. Know that thy careleſs Carriage has done more
Than all the Skill and diligence of Love
Could e're effeſt.

Sir Fred. What? the VVidow has ſome kind thoughts of my Body?

Beauf. She loves you, and dines on purpoſe at her Brother's houſe
This day, in hopes of ſeeing you.

Sir Fred. Some Women like Fiſhes deſpiſe the Bait,
Or elſe ſuſpeſt it, whilſt ſtill it's hobbing at
Their Mouths; but ſubtilly wav'd by the Angler's hand,
Greedily hang themſelves upon the Hook.

There

There are many so critically wise,
They'll suffer none to deceive them but themselves.

   Beauf. Cousin, 'tis time you were preparing for your Mistress.
   Sir Fred. Well, since 'tis my Fortune, I'll about it.
Widow thy Ruine lye upon thine own head :
Faith, my Lord you can witness,
'Twas none of my seeking.   [*Exeunt.*

SCENE III.

Scene *Wheadle*'s Lodging.

Enter Wheadle *and* Palmer.

   Whead. Come, bear thy Losses patiently.
   Palm. A Pox confound all Ordinaries,
If ever I play at an Ordinary agen —   [*Bites his Thumb.*
   Whead. Thou'lt lose thy Money :
Thou hast no power to forbear ;
I will as soon undertake to reclaim a Horse
From a Hitch he has learn'd in his Pace,
Or an old Mastive from worrying of Sheep.
   Palm. Ay, ay, there's nothing can do it but Hemp.
   Whead. Want of Money may do much.
   Palm. I protest I had rather still be vicious
Than owe my Virtue to Necessity.
How commendable is Chastity in an Eunuch ?
I am grown more than half virtuous, of late :
I have laid the dangerous Pad now quite aside ;
I walk within the Purlieus of the Law.
Could I but leave this Ordinary, this Square,
I were the most accomplisht Man in the Town.
   Whead. 'Tis pity thou art Master of thy Art ;
Such a nimble Hand, such neat Conveyance.
   Palm. Nay, I should have made an excellent Jugler, 'faith.
   Whead. Come, be cheerful,
I've lodg'd a Deer shall make amends for all ;
I lack'd a Man to help me set my Toyls,
And thou art come most happily.
   Palm. My dear *Wheadle*, who is it ?
   Whead. My new Friend, and Patron,
Sir *Nicholas Cully.*
   Palm. He's fat, and will say well, I promise you.
Well I'll do his business most dextrously,
Else let me ever lose the Honour

Of serving a Friend in the like Nature.

Whead. No more Words, but haſte, prepare for the Deſign;
Habit your ſelf like a good thrifty Countrey-man;
Get Tools, Dice and Money for the Purpoſe,
And meet me at the *Devil* about Three exactly.

Enter Boy.

Boy, Sir, Sir *Nicholas Cully* is without.

Whead. Deſire him to walk in.
Here, *Palmer,* the back Way, quickly, and be ſure————

Palm. Enough, enough, I'll warrant thee.   [Ex. Palm.

Enter Sir Nicholas Cully.

Whead. Sir *Nicholas,* this Viſit is too great a Favour:
I intended one to you;
How do you find your ſelf this Morning?

Cull. Faith, Much the dryer for the laſt nights wetting.

Whead. Like thirſty Earth which gapes the more
For a ſmall Shower;
We'll ſoak you throughly to day.

Cul. Excuſe me, Faith I am engag'd.

Whead. I am ſorry for't;
I meant you a ſhare in my good Fortune:
But ſince it cannot be————

Cul. What? What good Fortune?

Whead. Nay, 'twill but vex you to know it,
Since you have not leiſure to purſue it.

Cul. Dear *Wheadle,* prithee tell me.

Whead. Now do I want Power to keep it from you.
Juſt as you came in at that Door,
Went out at this a Waiting Gentlewoman,
Sent with a civil Meſſage from her Lady,
To deſire the Happineſs of my Company
This Afternoon, where I ſhould have the
Opportunity of ſeeing another lovely brisk Woman,
Newly married to a fooliſh Citizen,
Who will be apt enough to hear Reaſon,
From one that can ſpeak it better than her Husband:
I return'd my humble Thanks for the Honour ſhe did me,
And that I could not do my ſelf ſo great an Injury,
To diſobey her Will;
This is the Adventure;
But ſince y'ave Buſ'neſs————

Cul. A Pox on Buſ'neſs. I'll defer't.

Whead. By no means, for a ſilly Woman;
Our Pleaſures muſt be Slaves to our Affairs.

Cul. Were it to take Possession of an
Estate, I'd neglect it.
Are the Ladies Cavaliers?

Whead. Oh most Loyal-hearted Ladies!

Cul. How merry will we be then!

Whead. I say, mind your Bus'ness.

Cul. I'll go and put it off immediately.
Where shall I meet you in the Afternoon?

Whead. You'll find me at the *Devil* about Three
A Clock, where I expect a second Summons as
She passes toward the City.

Cul. Thither will I come without fail;
Be sure you wait for me   [*Ex.* Cully.

Cul. Wait for thee, as a Cat does for a Mouse
She intends to play with, and then prey upon.
How eagerly did this half-witted Fellow chap
Up the Bait? Like a ravenous Fish, that will
Not give the Angler leave to sink his Line,
But greedily darts up and meets it half way.   [*Ex. laughing.*

SCENE IV.

Scene the Lord Bevil's *House.*

Enter Graciana, *and* Aurelia *immediately after her, with a
Letter in her Hand.*

Grac. The Sun's grown lazy; 'tis a tedious space
Since he set forth, and yet's not half his Race.
I wonder *Beaufort* does not yet appear;
Love never loyters. Love sure brings him here.

Aur. Brought on the Wings of Love, here I present [*Presenting the Letter.*
His Soul, whose Body Prisons yet prevent;
The Noble *Bruce,* whose Vertues are his Crimes   [Grac. *rejects the Letter.*
Are you as false and cruel as the Times!
Will you not read the Stories of his Grief;
But wilfully refuse to give Relief?

Grac. Sister, from you this Language makes me start:
Can you suspect such Vices in my Heart?
His Vertues, I, as well as you, admire;
I never scorn'd, but pity much his Fire.

Aur. If you did pity, you would not reject [Grac. *rejects the Letter again.*
This Messenger of Love: This is Neglect.

Grac. 'Tis Cruelty to gaze on Wounds, I'm sure,
When we want Balsome to effect their Cure.

                                                        Aur

Aur. 'Tis only want of will in you, you have
Beauty to kill, and Virtue too to fave.

Grac. VVe of our felves can neither love nor hate;
Heav'n does referve the pow'r to guide our Fate.

Aurel. Graciana,——   *Enter Lord* Bevil, Lovis, *and the Widow.*

Grac. Sifter, forbear; my Father's here.

L. Bev. So Girl; what, no news of your Lover yet?
Our Dinner's ready, and I am afraid
He will go nigh to incur the Cooks anger.

Wid. I believe h'as undertook a hard task;
Sir *Frederick*, they fay, is no eafie man
To be perfwaded to come among us women.

Lov. Sir.   [Lovis *and Lord* Bevil *whifper.*

L. Bevil. VVhat now?

Wid. I am as impatient as thou art, Girl: [*To* Graciana.
I long to fee Sir *Frederick* here.

L. Bev. Forbear, I charge you on my blefling:
Not one word more of Colonel *Bruce.*

Lovis. You gave encouragement, Sir, to his Love;
The honour of our Houfe now lies at ftake.

L. Bev. You find by your Sifters inclinations
Heaven has decreed her otherwife.

Lovis. But Sir,——

L. Bev. Forbear to fpeak, or elfe forbear the Room.

Lovis. This I can obey, but not the other.   [*Exit* Lovis.

Enter Foot-boy.

Foot b. Sir, my Lord *Beaufort's* come.

L. Bev. 'Tis well.

Wid. D'hear, are there not two Gentlemen?

Foot-b. Yes, Madam, there is another proper handfom
Gentleman.   [*Exit Foot-boy.*

L. Bev. Come, let's walk in, and give them entertainment.

Wid. Now Coufin, for Sir *Frederick,* this man of men,
There's nothing like him.   [*Exeunt all but* Aurelia.

Aur. VVith curious diligence I ftill have ftrove   [*Holding the Letter in*
During your abfence, *Bruce,* to breathe your Love   *her hand.*
Into my Sifters bofom; But the fire
VVants force; Fate does againft my breath confpire:
I have obey'd, though I cannot fulfil,
Againft my felf, the dictates of your VVill;
My Love to yours do's yield; fince you enjoyn'd,
I hourly court my Rival to be kind;
VVith Paffion too, as great as you can do,
Taught by thofe wounds I have receiv'd from you.

C   Small

Small is the difference that's between our grief;
Yours finds no cure, and mine seeks no relief.
You unsuccessfully your Love reveal;
And I for ever must my Love conceal:
Within my bosom I'll your Letter wear,   *[Putting the Letter in her bosom.*
It is a Tomb that's proper for despair.   *[Exit.*

ACT II. SCENE I.

Scene, The Lord *Bevil's* House.

Enter Clark *and* Dusoy.

Clark. MEthinks the wound your Master gave you
Last night, makes you look very thin and
Wan, Monsieur.

Dusoy. Begar you are mistaké, it be de voundé
Dat my Metresse did give me long ago.

Clark. VVhat? some pretty little English Lady's
Crept into your heart?

Dusoy. No, but damn'd little English VVhore is creepé
Into my bone begar, me could vish dat de
Diable vould také her vid allé my harté.

Clark. You have manag'd your bus'ness ill, Mounsieur.

Dusoy. It vas de Raskal Cyrugin English dat did
Manage de business illé; me did putté my
Businessé into his haundé; he did stop de
Tapé, and de liquor did varké, varké, varké,
Up into de headé and de shoulder begar.

Clark. Like soap clapp'd under a Saddle.

Dusoy. Here come my Matré; holdé your peacé.   *[Ex. Clark.*

    Enter Sir Frederick, *Widow, and Maid.*

Sir. Fred. VVhither, whither do ye draw me, VVidow;
VVhat's your design?

Wid. To walk a turn in the Garden, and then
Repose in a cool Arbour.

Sir Fred. VVidow, I dare not venture my self in those amorous
Shades; you have a mind to be talking of Love
I perceive, and my heart's too tender to be trusted
VVith such conversation.

Wid. I did not imagine you were so foolishly
Conceited; is it your VVit or your Person, Sir,
That is so taking?

Sir Fred. Truly you are much miſtaken, I havé no
Such great thoughts of the young man you
See ; who ever knew a VVoman have ſo much
Reaſon to build her love upon merit ?
Have we not daily experience of great
Fortunes, that fling themſelves into the arms
Of vain idle Fellows ? Can you blame me then
For ſtanding upon my guard ? No, let us
Sit down here, have each on's a Bottle of VVine
At our elbows ; ſo prompted, I dare enter into
Diſcourſe with you.

Wid. VVou'd you have me ſit
And drink hand to fiſt with you, as if we were
In the *Fleece,* or ſome other of your beloved
Taverns ?

Sir Fred. Faith I wou'd have thee come as near
As poſſible to ſomething or other I have
Been us'd to converſe with, that I may
The better know how to entertain thee.

Wid. Pray which of thoſe Ladies you uſe to
Converſe with, could you fancy me to
Look like ? be merry, and tell me.

Sir Fred. 'Twere too great a ſin to compare thee
To any of them ; and yet th'aſt ſo incens'd
Me, I can hardly forbear to wiſh thee one
Of 'em. Ho, *Dufoy !*
VVidow, I ſtand in awe of this Gentleman ;
I muſt have his advice before I dare
Keep you Company any further.⸺ How de
You approve the ſpending of my time
VVith this Lady ?

Dufoy. Ver vel, Begar ;
I could viſh I had never ſpendé my time in de
Vorſé compaignie.

Wid. You look but ill, Monſieur ; have
You been ſick lately ?

Dufoy. I havé de ver great affliction in my mindé,
Madam.

Wid. VVhat is't ?

Dufoy. Truly I havé de ver great paſſion vor dis
Jentel woman, and ſhe have no compaſſion
At all vor me ; ſhe do refuſé me all my
Amouré and my adreſſé.

Wid. Indeed *Betty* you are too blame.

Maid. Out upon him for a French diſſembler,
He never ſpake to me in his life, Madam.

Dufoy. You ſee, Madam, ſhe ſcorné me vor
Her Serviteur.

Maid. Pray, when did you make any of your French
Lové to mé?

Dufoy. It vil breké my hearté to remember de
Time ven you did refuſé mé?

Wid. Will you permit me to ſerve you in this
Buſineſs, Monſieur.

Dufoy. Madam, it be d' honour vor de King dé
France.

Wid. Betty, whither run you?

Maid. I'll not ſtay to be jeer'd by a ſneaking
Valet-de-Chambré: I'll be reveng'd
If I live, Monſieur.

Wid. I'll take ſome other time.

Dufoy. Van you have de leiſuré, Madam.

Sir Fred. By thoſe lips, ――――

Wid. Nay pray forbear, Sir.

Sir Fred. Who's conceited now, Widow? cou'd
You imagine I was ſo fond to kiſs them?

Wid. You cannot blame me for ſtanding on
My guard ſo near an Enemy.

Sir Fred. If you are ſo good at that, Widow,
Let's ſee, what guard wou'd you chuſe to be at,
Shou'd the Trumpet ſound a Charge
To this dreadful Foe?

Wid. It is an idle Queſtion amongſt experienc'd
Souldiers; but if we ever have a War,
We'll never trouble the Trumpet; the
Bells ſhall proclaim our Quarrel.

Sir Fred. It will be moſt proper; they ſhall be
Rung backwards.

Wid. Why ſo, Sir?

Sir Fred. I'll have all the helps that may be to
Allay a dangerous fire; Widows muſt
Needs have furious flames; the Bellows
Have been at work, and blown 'em up.

Wid. You grow too rude, Sir: I will have my
Humour, a walk i' th' Garden; and afterwards
We'll take the Air in the Park.

Sir Fred. Let us join hands then, Widow.

Wid. Without the dangerous help of a Parſon.

I do not fear it, Sir.   [*Ex*. Sir Fred. *and* Wid.

Dufoy. Begar, I do not care two Soulz if de
Shamber-maid ver hangé; be it not
Great deal better pretendé d' affection to
Her, dan to tellé de hole Varldé I do take
De Medicine vor de clapé ? begar it
Be de ver great deale better.   [*Ex*. Dufoy.

SCENE II.

Scene, A Garden belonging to my Lord *Bevill's* House.

Enter Beaufort *and* Graciana.

Beauf. Graciana, why do you condemn your Love ?
Your Beauty without that, alas ! would prove
But my deftruction, an unlucky Star,
Prognofticating ruine and defpair.
  Grac. Sir, you miftake ; 'tis not my Love I blame,
But my Difcretion ; * Here the active flame   [* *Pointing to her Breaft.*
Shou'd yet a longer time have been conceal'd,
Too foon, too foon I fear it was reveal'd.
Our weaker Sex glories in a Surprize,
We boaft the fudden Conquefts of our Eyes ;
But men efteem a Foe that dares contend,
One that with noble Courage does defend
A wounded Heart ; the Victories they gain
They prize by their own hazard and their pain.
  Beauf. Graciana, can you think we take delight
To have our happinefs againft us fight ;
Or that fuch goodnefs fhou'd us men difpleafe
As do's afford us Heav'n with greater cafe ?
        [*Enter* Lovis, *walking difcontentedly.*
See where your Brother comes ; his
Carriage has been ftrange of late to me ;
I never gave him caufe of difcontent ;
He takes no notice of our being here :
I will falute him.
  Grac. By no means ;
Some ferious thoughts you fee employ his mind.
  Beauf. I muft be civil. Your Servant, Sir.
  Lov. You are my Sifters Servant, Sir ; go fawn.
Upon your Miftrefs ; Fare-you-well.   [*Ex*. Lovis.
  Beauf. Fare-you-well, if you are no better Company.

Heavens !

[Grac. *weep*

Heavens! what is the matter?
VVhat faucy forrow dares approach your heart?
VVaste not thefe precious Tears; Oh, weep no more,
Shou'd Heav'n frown, the world wou'd be too poor,
(Rob'd of the facred Treafure of your eyes)
To pay for mercy one fit Sacrifice.
  "*Grac.* My Brother, Sir, is growing mad, I fear.
  Beauf. Your Brother is a man whofe noble Mind
VVas to fevereft Virtue ftill inclin'd;
He in the School of Honour has been bred,
And all her fubtle Laws with heed has read:
There is fome hidden caufe, I fain would know
From whence thefe ftrange diforders in him flow.
Graciana, fhall I beg you to difpel
Thefe Mifts which round my troubl'd Reafon dwell.
  Grac. It is a Story I cou'd wifh you'd learn
From one whom it does not fo much concern;
I am th' unhappy caufe of what y'ave feen;
My Brother's Paffion does proceed from mine.
  Beauf. This does confound me more; it cannot be;
You are the joy of all your Family:
Dares he condemn you for a noble love,
VVhich honour and your duty both approve.
  Grac. My Lord, thofe errors merit our excufe
VVhich an accefs of virtue does produce.
  Beauf. I know that envy is too bafe a gueft
To have a lodging in his generous breaft;
'Tis fome extream of Honour, or of Love,
Or both, that thus his indignation move.
  Grac. E're I begin, you my fad ftory end;
You are a Rival to his deareft Friend.
  Beauf. Graciana, though you have fo great a fhare
Of Beauty, all that fee you Rivals are;
Yet during this fmall fpace I did proclaim,
To you, and to the world, my purer flame,
I never faw the Man that durft draw near,
VVith his ambitious Love t'affault your Ear.
VVhat providence has kept us thus afunder?
  Grac. VVhen I have fpoke you'l find it is no wonder.
He has a Miftrefs more renown'd than me,
VVhom he does Court, his dearer Loyalty;
He on his legs does now her favours wear;
He is confin'd by her foul Ravifher:
You may not know his Perfon; but his Name

Is strange to none that have convers'd with Fame:
'Tis *Bruce*.

   Beauf. The Man indeed I ne're did see,
But have heard wonders of his Gallantry.

   Grac. This gallant Man my Brother ever lov'd;
But his Heroick Virtues so improv'd
In time those seeds of Love which first were sown,
That to the highest Friendship they are grown.
This Friendship first, and not his Love to me,
Sought an Alliance with our Family.
My Sister and my self were newly come
From learning how to live, to live at home;
VVhen barren of discourse one day, and free
VVith's Friend, my Brother chanc'd to talk of me;
Unlucky accident! his Friend reply'd;
He long had wish'd their Blood might be ally'd;
Then press'd him that they might my Father move
To give an approbation to his Love:
His Person and his merits were so great,
He granted faster than they could entreat;
He wish'd the Fates that govern hearts wou'd be
So kind to him to make our hearts agree,
But told them he had made a sacred Vow,
Never to force what Love should disallow.

                         [*Enter Sir* Frederick *and Widow.*

But see, Sir *Frederick* and my Aunt.
My Lord, some other time I will relate
The story of his Love, and of its Fate.

   Sir Fred. How now my Lord? so grave a countenance
In the presence of your Mistress?
VVidow, what wou'd you give
Your eyes had power to make me such
Another melancholly Gentleman?

   Wid. I have seen e'ne as merry a man as
Your self, Sir *Frederick*, brought to stand
VVith folded arms, and with a tristful look
Tell a mournful tale to a Lady.

                  [*Enter a Foot-boy, and whispers Sir* Frederick.

   Sir Fred. The Devil owes some men a shame;
The Coach is ready; VVidow, I know
You are ambitious to be seen in my Company.

   Wid. My Lord, and Cousin, will you honour
Me with yours to the Park; that may take off the
Scandal of his?

                                  Enter

Enter Aurelia *and* Leticia.

Beauf. Madam, we'll wait upon you;
But we muſt not leave this Lady behind us.

Wid. Couſin *Aurelia* ——

Aurel. Madam, I beg you will excuſe me, and
You, my Lord; I feel a little indiſpoſition,
And dare not venture into ſo ſharp an
Air.

Beauf. Your Servant, Madam.   [*Exeunt all but* Aurelia *and* Leticia.

Aurel. Retire; I wou'd not have you ſtay with me,
I have too great a train of miſery.
If virtuous Love in none be cauſe of ſhame,
Why ſhou'd it be a crime to own the flame?
But we by Cuſtom, not by Nature led,
Muſt in the beaten paths of Honour tread.
I love thee *Bruce*; but Heav'n, what have I done!
Leticia, did I not command you hence?

Letic. Madam, I hope my care is no offence:
I am afflicted thus to ſee you take
Delight to keep your miſeries awake.

Aurel. Since you have heard me, ſwear you will be true;
Leticia, none muſt know I love but you.

Letic. If I at any time your Love declare,
May I of Heav'n and ſerving you deſpair.
Though I am young, yet I have felt this ſmart;
Love once was buſie with my tender heart.

Aurel. Wert thou in love?

Letic. I was.

Aurel. Prethee, with whom?

Letic. With one that like my ſelf did newly bloom:
Methoughts his Actions were above his years.   [*She weeps.*

Aurel. Leticia, you confirm me by your tears;
Now I believ'd you lov'd; did he love you?

Letic. That had been more than to my Love was due;
He was ſo much above my humble Birth,
My Paſſion had been fitter for his Mirth.

Aurel. And does your Love continue ſtill the ſame?

Letit. Some ſparks remain, but time has quencht the flame;
I hope 'twill prove as kind to you, and cure
Theſe greater griefs which (Madam) you endure.

Aurel. Time to my bleeding heart brings no relief;
Death there muſt heal the fatal wounds of grief:
Leticia, come, within this ſhady Bower
We'll join our mournful Voices, and repeat
The ſaddeſt tales we ever learn'd of Love.

                                             Aurelia

Aurelia and Leticia walk into an Arbour, and sing this Song in Parts.

SONG.

When Phillis *watch'd her harmless Sheep,*
  Not one poor Lamb was made a Prey;
Yet she had cause enough to weep,
  Her silly Heart did go astray:
Then flying to the neighbouring Grove,
She left her tender Flock to rove,
And to the Winds did breathe her Love.
    She sought in vain
    To ease her Pain;
The heedless Winds did fan her Fire;
    Venting her Grief
    Gave no Relief;
But rather did increase Desire.
Then sitting with her Arms a-cross,
  Her Sorrows streaming from each Eye;
She fixt her Thoughts upon her Loss,
  And in Despair resolv'd to dye.

Aurel. Why should you weep, *Leticia,* whilst we sing? ⎰*Walking out of*
Tell me, from whence those gentle Currents spring? ⎱ *the Arbour.*
Can yet your faded Love cause such Fresh Showers?
This Water is too good for dying Flowers.

Letic. Madam, it is such Love commands this Dew,
As cannot fade; it is my Love to you.

Aurel. Leticia, I am weary of this place;
And yet I know not whither I should go.

Letic. Will you be pleas'd to try if you can sleep?
That may deceive you of your cares a while.

Aurel. I will: there's nothing here does give me ease,
But in the End will nourish my Disease.   [*Exeunt.*

SCENE III.

Scene, *A Tavern.*

Enter Wheadle, *and immediately after him a* Foot-Boy.

Whead. The Hour is come;
Where's your Master, Sirrah?
Foot-B. He'll be here immediately, Sir.

Whead.

Whead. Is he neatly dress'd?

Boy. In the very suit he won the other day
Of the *Buckingham-*shire Grasier.

Whead. Take this Letter, and give it me
VVhen you perceive me talking with
Sir *Nicholas Cully,* with Recommendations from a Lady;
Lurk in some secret Place till he's come,
That he may not perceive you at his Entrance.
Oh here's *Palmer.*   [*Ex.* Foot-boy.

Thom, what's the Price of a Score of fat   [*Enter* Palmer.
VVeathers?

Palm. Do they not well become me, Boy?

Whead. Nature doubtless intended thee for a Rogue,
She has so well contrived thee for Disguises.
Here comes Sir *Nicholas.*   [*Enter Sir* Nicholas.
Sir *Nicholas,* Come, come; this is an honest Friend
And Country man of mine.

Sir *Nich.* Your Servant, Sir; Is not the Lady come by yet?

Whead. I expect her every moment,——Ho, here's her Boy.
Well, what News?   [*Enter* Boy.

Boy. My Lady presents her Service to you, Sir,
And has sent you this.   [*Delivers a Letter.*

[*Wheadle reads, and seems much displeas'd.*

Sir *Nich.* What is the matter, Man?

Whead. Read, read; I want Patience to tell you. [*Gives* Cul. *the Letter.*
Fortune still jades me in all my Expectations.

Sir *Nich. reading the Letter.* The Citizen's Wife forc'd
To go to *Greenwich* with her Husband;
Will meet some time next Week.
Come, come, *Wheadle,* another time will do;
Be not so passionate, Man!

Whead. I must abuse my Friend upon an idle
Woman's VVords!

Sir *Nich.* Pish, 'tis an Accident: Come, let us
Drink a Glass of Wine, to put these Women
Out of our Heads.

Palm. Women? Ho Boys, Women, where are the Women?

Whead. Here's your merry Countrey-man.

Palmer *sings.*

He took her by the Apron,
To bring her to his Beck;
But as he wound her to him,
The Apron-strings did break.

Enter

Enter Drawer *with Wine.*

Sir Nich. A merry man indeed, Sir, my Service to you. [*Drinks to* Pal.

Palm. Thank you, Sir. Come Mr. *Wheadle,* remembring
My Land-lord, i'faith ; wou'd he were e'en among us now.
Come, be merry man. * Lend me your hand, Sir ; you   [* *To Sir* Nich.
Look like an honeſt man ; here's a good health to all
That are ſo: Tope —— here pledge me.   [*Drinks.*
                       [*Gives Sir* Nicholas *the Glaſs.*

Sir Nich. Mr. *Wheadle,* to you   [*Drinks and leaves ſome in the Glaſs.*
Palm. I'll not abate you an ace. 'Slid, y' are not
So honeſt as I took you for.   [Sir Nicholas *drinks up the reſt.*

Palmer *Sings.*

> *If any man baulk his Liquor,*
> *Let him never baulk the Gallows,*
> *But ſing a Pſalm there wi' th' Vicar,*
> *Or die in a dirty Ale-houſe.*

Enter Drawer.

Drawer. There's a Country-man below
Deſires to ſpeak with his Maſter. *Palmer.*

Palm. So, ſo, thank thee Lad ; it is my man,
I appointed him to call here ; h'as ſold the Cattle,
I warrant you : I'll wait on you agen preſently,
Gentlemen.   [*Exit* Palmer.

Whead. Is not this a very pleaſant Fellow ?
Sir Nich. The pleaſanteſt I ever met with ; what is he ?
Whead. He's a *Buckingham-ſhire* Grazier, very rich ;
He has the fat Oxen, and fat Acres in the Vale :
I met him here by chance, and could not avoid
Drinking a Glaſs o' Wine with him. I believe,
He's gone down to receive Money ;
'Twere an excellent deſign to bubble him.
Sir Nich. How 'twou'd change his merry Note ;
Will you try him ?
Whead. Do you ; I cannnot appear in't,
Becauſe he takes me for his Friend.
Sir Nich. How neatly I could top upon him !
Whead. All things will paſs upon him,
I'll go your half: Talk of Dice,
You'll perceive if he's coming.
What Money have you about you ?
Sir Nich. Ten Pieces.

                D 2   *Whead.*

Whead. I have about that quantity too, here, take it,
If he should run us out of our ready Money,
Be sure you set him deep upon Tick,
If he'll be at you, that we may recover it;
For we'll not pay a Farthing of what we lose that way,
Hush, here he comes.

   Enter Palmer with a Bag of Money under his Arm, and flings it
                    upon the Table.

   Palm. All my fat Oxen and Sheep are melted to this,
Gentlemen.

   Whead. Their Grease is well try'd, Sir.

   Sir Nich. Come, Sir, for all your Riches,
You are in Arrear here.　　　　　　　　　　　　　[*Offers him a Glass.*

   Palm. I'll be soon out of your Debts:
My hearty Love to you, Sir.　　　　　　　　　　　[*Drinks.*
Wou'd I had you both in *Buckingham-shire*,
And a Pipe of this Canary in my Cellar;
We'd roast an Ox before we parted;
Shou'd we not, Boy?

              Palmer *Sings.*

     We'd sing, and we'd laugh, and we'd drink all the Day;
     Our Reason we'd banish, our Senses shou'd sway;
     And every Pleasure our Wills shou'd obey.

   Palm. Come, drink to me a Brimmer if you
Dare now.

   Sir Nich. Nay, if you provoke me you'd find me a bold Man:
Give me a bigger Glass, Boy, So,
This is fit for Men of Worship; Hang your Retail Drinkers;
Have at thee, my brave Country-man.　　　　　　　[*Drinks.*

   Palm. I'll do all I can for my guts to pledge thee.
Ho brave Boys! that's he, that's he, 'faith,
How I cou'd hug thee now! Mr. *Wheadle*, to you.

   Whead. I protest, Gentlemen, you'll fright me
Out of your Company. Sir *Nicholas*,
Shall we have th' other round?

   Sir Nich. Let's pause a while. What say you,
Gentlemen, if, to pass away the time,
And to refresh us, we should have a Box and Dice,
And fling a merry Mayn among our selves in sport?

   Whead. 'Twill spoil good Company; by no means, Sir *Nicholas.*

   Palm. Hang Play among Friends; let's have a Wench.

                            Sings

Sings.

And, Jenny was all my Joy,
She had my Heart at her will;
But I left her and her toy
When once I had got my fill.

What say you, shall we have her?
Sir Nich. We are not enough drunk for a Wench:
Palm. Let's sing a Catch then.
Whead. Cull. Agreed, agreed.
Whead. Begin, Mr. *Palmer.*

Palmer sings, standing in the middle, with a Glass of Wine in his hand.
Palm. I have no design here,
But drinking good Wine here.
Whea. *Nor I Boy.*
Sir Nich. *Nor I, Boy.*
Whea. *Th' art my Boy.*
Sir Nich. *Th' art my Boy.*
All 3. *Our heads are too airy for Plots:*
Let us hug then all three,
Since our Virtues agree,
We'll hollow and cast up our Hats.

[*They hollow whi'st* Palmer *drinks, and then*
change till it has gone round.

Sir Nich. Enough, enough.
Palm. Very good Boys all, very good Boys all.
Give me a Glass of Wine there; fill a Brimmer,
Sir *Nicholas*, your Lady.
Sir Nich. Pray, Sir, forbear; I must be forc'd to leave
Your Company else. Prithee, *Wheadle*,
Let's have a Box and Dice.
Whead. We shall grow dull. Mr. *Palmer*,
What say you to the Bus'ness?
Palm. I don't understand Dice; I understand good Pasture
And Drink—— Hang the Devil's Bones.

[Wheadle *whispers* Cully *to send for Dice.*
Cully *whispers the* Drawer.

Palmer *Sings.*
He that leaves his Wine for Boxes and Dice,
Or his Wench for fear of Mishaps,
May he beg all his days, cracking of Lice,
And die in Conclusion of Claps.

Enter

Enter Drawer *with Dice.*

Palm. Come, come, Gentlemen, this is the harmleſſer
Sport of the two ; a merry Glaſs round.

Sir Nich. Excuſe me, Sir, I'll pledge you here.   [*Takes Dice.*
Come, come, Sir, on Six ; Six is the Main ?

Palm. The Main, what's the Main ?

Sir Nich. Do not you underſtand Hazard ?

Palm. I underſtand Dice, or Hap-Hazard.

Sir Nich. Can you play at Paſſage ?

Palm. You paſs my Underſtanding : I can fling
Moſt at a throw, for a Shot, or a Glaſs of Wine.

Sir Nich. Paſſage is eaſily learn'd : The Caſtor wins,
If he fling above ten with Doublets
Upon three Dice.

Palm. How Doublets ?

Sir Nich. Two of a ſort, two Cinques, two Tre's, or the like.

Palm. Ho, ho, I have you.

Sir Nich. Come, ſet then.

Palm. I ſet you this Bottle.

Sir Nich. Nay, nay, ſet Money.

Palm. Is it a fair play, Mr. *Wheadle* ? I truſt to you.

Whead. Upon my word a very fair ſquare Play,
But this Table is ſo wet, there's no playing upon it.

Drawer. will you be pleas'd to remove into the next Room,
Gentlemen ?

Sir Nich. I think it will not be amiſs.

Whead. Much better. Come, Mr. *Palmer.*

Palm. I'll follow, Sir.

Palmer *Sings.*

> *If ſhe be not as kind as fair,*
> *But peeviſh and unhandy,*
> *Leave her, ſhe's only worth the care*
> *Of ſome ſpruce Jack-a dandy.*
> *I wou'd not have thee ſuch an Aſs,*
> *Had'ſt thou ne're ſo much Leiſure,*
> *To ſigh and whine for ſuch a Laſs,*
> *Whoſe Pride's about her Pleaſure.*

Sir Nich. Ho brave Boy.

Palm. March on, march on.

Sings.

SINGS.

Make much of e'ry buxome Girl,
Which needs but little Courting;
Her Value is above the Pearl,
That takes Delight in Sporting.

[*Ex. Omnes.*

ACT III. SCENE I.

Scene, A Tavern.

Enter Sir Nicholas Cully, Wheadle, Palmer, *and Drawer.*

Palm. NAY, Sir *Nich'las*, for all your hafte, I muft
Have a Note under your Hand for the thoufand
Pounds you owe me.

Whead. This muft not be among Friends, Mr. *Palmer*;
Sir *Nich'las* fhall not pay the Money.

Sir Nich. I had been a Mad-man to play at fuch a Rate
If I had ever intended to pay.

Palm. Though I am but a poor Country-man,
I fcorn to be chous'd : I have Friends in Town.

Whead. But hark you, Mr. *Palmer* ?

Palm. Hark me no Harks; I'll have my Money.

Sir Nich. Drawer, take your Reck'ning.

Whead. laughing. Farewel, Sir; hafte into the Countrey
To mind your Cattle.

Palm. But hark you, Gentlemen; are you in earneft?

Whead. Ay indeed; Fare you well, Sir.

Palm. I took you for my Friend, Mr. *Wheadle*;
But now I perceive what you are.
* Your Ear, Sir.   [* *To* Cully.

Whead. Never fear him; he dares not go into the Field,
Without it be among his Sheep.

Cul. Agreed; To morrow, about Eight in the Morning,
Near *Pancridge*.

Whead. I will have the Honour to ferve you, Sir *Nich'las*.
Provide your felf a Second, Mr. *Palmer*.

[*Exeunt Sir* Nich. *and* Wheadle *laughing.*

Palm. So, Laugh:
This is the Sheep that I muft fleece.   [*Exit.*

SCENE

SCENE II.

Scene, Covent-Garden.

Enter Sir Fredrick Frollick *, with Fidlers before him, and six or eight Link Boys, dancing and singing.*

Sir Fred. Here, here, this is the Window;
Range your selves here.

Enter the Bell-Man.

Bell-M Good morrow, Gentlemen.
Sir Fred. Honeft Bell-Man, prithee lend me thy Bell.
Bell-M. With all my Heart, Mafter.
　　　　　　　　　[*Sir* Fred. *rings the Bell and then repeats thefe Verfes.*
Sir Fred. *You, Widow, that do sleep Dog-sleep,*
　　　　And now for your dead Husband weep,
　　　　Perceiving well what want you have
　　　　Of that poor Worm has eat in Grave;
　　　　Rife out of Bed, and ope the Door;
　　　　Here's that will all your Joys reftore.
　　　　Good-morrow, my Miftrefs dear, Good-morrow.
　　　　Good morrow, Widow.　　　　[*He rings the Bell again.*
　　The Chamber-maid comes to the Window unlac'd, holding her
　　　　　　　Petticoats in her Hand.
Maid. Who's that comes at this unfeafonable Hour,
To difturb my Ladies Quiet?
Sir Fred. An honeft *Bell-Man,* to mind her of her Frailty.
Maid. Sir *Frederick,* I wonder you will offer this;
You will lofe her Favour for ever.
Sir Fred. Y' are miftaken; now's the Time to creep into
Her Favour.
Maid. I'm fure y'ave wak'd me out of the fweeteft Sleep:
Hey ho———
Sir Fred. Poor Girl! Let me in, I'll rock
Thee into a fweeter.
Maid. I hear a ftirring in my Miftreffes Chamber;
I believe y'ave frighted her.　·　　　　　　[*Ex.* Maid.
Sir Fred. Sound a frefh Alarm; the Enemy's at hand.　[*Fidlers play.*
　　　　　[*The Widow comes to the Window in her Night Gown.*
Wid. Whofe Infolence is this, that dares affront me
Thus?
Sir Fred. in ⎱ If there be Infolence in Love, 'tis I
a Canting Tone. ⎰ Have done you this unwilling Injury.

　　　　　　　　　　　　　　　　　　　　Wid

Wid. What pitiful rhyming Fellow's that? he speaks
As if he were prompted by the Fidlers.

Sir Fred. Alas, what pains I take thus to unclose
Those pretty Eye-lids which lock'd up my Foes!

Wid. A godly Buke would become that tone a great
Deal better: He might get a pretty living by
Reading Mother *Shipton's* Prophecies, or some
Pious Exhortation at the corner of a Street:
His mournful Voice, I vow, has mov'd my compassion.

Sir Fred. Ay, ay, we shou'd have a Fellow-feeling of one
Another indeed, Widow.

Wid. Sir *Frederick*, is it you?

Sir Fred. Yes truly; and can you be angry, Lady?
Have not your Quarters been beaten up
At these most seasonable hours before now?

Wid. Yes; but it has been by one that has had a Commission
For what he did: I'm afraid shou'd it once become
Your Duty, you would soon grow weary of the Employment.

Sir Fred. Widow, I hate this distance; 'tis not the English fashion:
Prethee let's come to't hand to fist.

Wid. I give no entertainment to such lewd persons.
Farewel, Sir.   [*Exit Wid.*

Sir Fred. I'll fetch thee again, or conjure the whole Garden up.
Sing the Catch I taught you at the *Rose*.   [*Fidlers sing.*

SONG.

HE that will win a Widows Heart
  Must bear up briskly to her:
She loves the Lad that's free and smart,
But hates the formal Wooer.

Widow runs to the Window again, with her Maid.

Wid. Hold, hold, Sir *Frederick*; what do you imagine
The Neighbours will think?

Sir Fred. So ill, I hope, of thee, thou'lt be forc'd to
Think the better of me.

Wid. I am much beholden to you for the care you have
Of my Reputation.

Sir Fred. Talk no more, but let the door be open'd;
Or else Fidlers ——

Wid. Pray hold; what security shall I have for
Your good behaviour?

Sir Fred. My Sobriety.

E   *Wid.*

Wid. That's pawn'd at the Tavern from whence
You came.

    Sir *Fred.* Thy own Honesty then; is that engag'd?

    Wid. I think that will go nigh to secure me.

Give 'em entrance, *Betty*   [*Ex Widow and her Maid.*

Enter Palmer, *with a Link before him.*

    Sir *Fred.* Ha! who goes there?

    Palm. An humble Creature of yours, Sir.

    Sir *Fred.* *Palmer* in a disguise! what roguery
Hast thou been about?

    Palm. Out of my loyal inclinations doing
Service to his Majesty.

    Sir *Fred.* What? a plotting?

    Palm. How to destroy his Enemies, Mr. *Wheadle*
And I are very vigilant.

    Sir *Fred.* In bubbling of some body, on my life.

    Palm. We do not use to boast our services,
Nor do we seek Rewards; good actions
Recompence themselves.

    Sir *Fred.* Ho the door opens; farewel, Sirrah.
Gentlemen, wait you without, and be ready
When I call.
Honest Bell-man, drink this.   [*Gives the Bell-man money.*

    Bell-m. Thank you, Noble Master.   [*Exit Bell man.*

    Sir *Fred. entring.* Here's something to stop thy mouth too.

                 [*The Maid shrieks.*

    Maid. Out upon you, Sir *Frederick*; you'l never leave
Your old tricks.   [*Exeunt.*

SCENE III.

Scene, The Widow's House.

Enter Sir Frederick, *leading the Widow, follow'd by her Maid.*

    Sir *Fred.* Little did I think I shou'd have been brought
To this pass: Love never had the power to rob me
Of my rest before.

    Wid. Alas poor Gentleman! he has not been us'd to
These late hours.

    Sir *Fred.* Widow, do not you be peevish now; 'tis dangerous
Jesting with my affection; 'tis in its infancy, and
Must be humour'd.

    Wid. Pray teach me how, Sir.

    Sir *Fred.* Why, with kisses, and such pretty little dalliances;
Thus, thus.   [*Kisses her.*
                                    Wid.

Wid. Hold, hold, Sir ; if it be so froward, put it out
To Nurse ; I am not so fond of it as you imagine ;
Pray how have you difpos'd of your brave Camerades ?
Have you left them to the mercy of the Beadle ?

Sir *Fred.* No, you muft be acquainted with their Virtues.
Enter, Gentlemen.

*Enter the Fidlers, and a Mafque of the Link boys, who are Dancing-
mafters, difguis'd for the Frollick.*

Wid. Thefe are men of skill.   [*After the Mafque.*

Sir *Fred.* I difguis'd 'em for your Entertainment.

Wid. Well, Sir, now I hope you'l leave me to my
Reft.

Sir *Fred.* Can you in confcience turn a young man
Out of doors at this time o' th' night, Widow ?
Fie, fie, the very thought on't will keep you
VVaking.

Wid. So pretty, fo well-favour'd a young man ;
One that loves me.

Sir *Fred.* Ay, one that loves you.

Wid. Truly 'tis a very hard hearted thing.   [*She fighs.*

Sir *Fred.* Come, come be mollifi'd. You may go, Gentlemen,
And leave me here ; you may go.   [*To the Mafquers.*

Wid. You may ftay, Gentlemen ; you may ftay,
And take your Captain along with you :
You'l find good Quarters in fome warm Hay-loft.

Sir *Fred.* Mercilefs VVoman! Do but lend me thy Maid ; Faith I'll
Ufe her very tenderly and lovingly, even as I'd ufe
Thy felf, dear VVidow, if thou wou'dft but make proof
Of my affection.

Wid. If the Conftable carry your fufpicious perfon to the
Compter, pray let me have notice of it ; I'll fend my
Taylor to be your Bail.

Sir *Fred.* Go, go to Bed, and be idle, VVidow ; that's worfe than
Any misfortune I can meet with. Strike up, and give
Notice of our coming. Farewel, VVidow ;
I pity thy folitary condition.   [*Exeunt Fidlers playing.*

SCENE IV.

Scene, Sir *Frederick's* Lodging.

Enter Dufoy, *and* Clark.

Clark. I wonder Sir *Frederick* ftays out fo late.

Dufoy. Dis is noting ; fix, feven a Clock in the morning

Is ver good hour.

Clark. I hope he does not ufe thefe hours often.

Dufoy. Some fix, feven times a Veek ; no oftiner.

Clark. My Lord commanded me to wait his coming.

Dufoy. Matré Clark, to divertife you, I vil tell you
How I did get be acquainted vid dis bedlam Matre.
About two, tree year ago, me had for my conveniance   [*Enter a Foot-boy.*
Difchargé my felf from attending as Matré D'oftel to
A perfon of Condition in *Parie* ; it hapen after de
Difpatch of my little affairé ———

Foot.b. That is, after h'ad fpent his money, Sir.

Dufoy. Jan foutré de Lacque ; me vil have de Vip
And de Belle vor your breeck, Rogue.

Foot.b. Sir, in a word, he was *Jack-pudding* to a Mountebank,
And turn'd off for want of Wit : my Mafter pick'd him
Up before a Puppit-fhow, mumbling a half-penny
Cuftard, to fend him with a Letter to the Poft.

Dufoy. Morbleu, fee, fee de infolance of de Foot-boy Englifh,
Bogre Rafcale, you lye, begar I vil cutté your troaté.   [*Exit Foot boy.*

Clark. He's a Rogue ; on with your ftory, Monfieur.

Dufoy. Matré Clark, I am your ver humble Serviteur ; but
Begar me have no patience to be abufé.   As I did fay, After
De difpatché of my affairé, van day being Idele, vich
Does producé de Mellanchollique, I did valké over
De new Bridge in *Parie*, and to devertife de time,
And my more ferious toughté, me did look to fee
De Marrioneté and de Jack-puddingé, vich
Did play hundred pretty triké, time de
Collation vas come ; and vor I had no company, I vas
Unvilling to go to de Cabareté, but did buy a Darriolé,
Littel Cuftardé vich did fatisfie my apetite ver vel :
In dis time young Mounfieur de *Grandvil* (a Jentelman
Of ver great Quality, van dat vas my ver good Friendé,
And has done me ver great and infignal faveure)
Come by in his Caroché, vid dis Sir *Frollick*, who did
Pention at the fame Academy, to learn de
Language, de bon mine, de great horfe, and
Many oder triké : Monfieur feeing me did
Make de bowé, and did beken, beken me come
To him : he did tellé me dat de Englis Jentelman
Had de Letré vor de Pofté, and did entreaté
Me (if I had de oppertunity) to fee de Letré
Deliver : he did tellé me too, it vold be ver great
Obligation : de memory of de faveur I had

Receive

Receive from his Famelyé, befide de inclination I
Naturally have to fervé de ftrangeré, made me
Returné de complemen vid ver great civility,
And fo I did take de Letré, and fee it deliveré.
Sir *Frollick* perceiving (by de management of dis
Affairé) dat I vas man d'efprit, and of vitté, did
Entreaté me to be his Serviteur; me did take
D'affection to his Perfoné, and vas contenté to live
Vid him, to counfel and to advifé him. You fee
Now a Eye of the Bougre dé Lacque Englifhé, Morbleu.

Enter a Foot-man.

Foot m. Monfieur, the Apothecary is without.

Dufoy. Dat news be no ver velcome, begar.
Matré Clark, go and fit you down; I vil but fwal
My Break face, and be vid you again prefant.
Morbleu L' Apothecaré.

SCENE V.

Scene, A Field.

Enter Wheadle *and* Cully.

Cully. Dear *Wheadle*, this is too dangerous a teftimony
Of thy kindnefs.

Whead. I fhou'd be angry with you if you thought fo:
What makes you fo ferious?

Cul. I am forry I did not provide for both our fafeties

Whead. How fo?

Cul. Colonel *Hewfon* is my Neighbour, and very good
Friend; I might have acquainted him with
The bufinefs, and got him with a File of
Musketiers to fecure us all.

Whead. But this wou'd not fecure your Honour.
What wou'd the World have judg'd?

Cul. Let the World have judg'd what it wou'd: Have
We not had many precedents of late, and
The World knows not what to judge?

Whead. But you fee there was no need to hazard
Your Reputation; here's no Enemy appears.

Cul. We have done our duty, let's be going then.

VVhead. We ought to wait a while.

Cul. The air is fo bleak, I vow I can no longer
Endure it.

VVhead. Have a little patience, methinks I fee two

Making towards us
In the next Clofe.

Cul. Where, where? 'tis them.

Whead. Bear up bravely now like a Man.

Cul. I proteft I am the worft diffembler
In cafes of this nature.

Whead. Alon; look like a Man of refolution.
Whither, whither go you?

Cul. But to the next Houfe to make my Will,
For fear of the worft : tell them I'll be here
Again prefently.

Whead. By no means; if you give 'em the leaft occafion
To fufpect you, they'l appear like Lyons.

Cul. Well, 'tis but giving fecurity for the money;
That will bring me off at laft..

Enter Palmer and his Second.

Palm. I fee you ride the Fore-horfe, Gentlemen.

[*All ftrip but* Cully, *who fumbles with his Doublet.*

Whead. Good-morrow, Sir.

Sec. Come, Sir, let us match the Swords.   [*To* Wheadle.

Whead. With all my heart.   [*They match the Swords.*

Palmer *Sings.*

> *He had and a good right* Bilbo *blade,*
> *Wherewith he us'd to vapour ;*
> *Full many a stubborn Foe had made*
> *To wince and cut a caper.*

Sec. Here's your Sword, Sir.   [*To* Palmer.

Palm. Come, Sir, are you ready for this fport?   [*To* Cully.

Cul. By and by, Sir; I will not rend the buttons from my
Doublet for no mans pleafure.

Whead. Death, y'ave fpoil'd all; make hafte.

Cul. Hang 'em, the Devil eggs 'em on; they will fight.

Palm. What, will you never have done fumbling?

Sec. This is a fhame; fight him with his Doublet on;
There's no foul play under it.

Palm. Come, Sir, have at you.   [*Making to* Cully.

Sec. Here, here, Sir.   [*To* Wheadle.

Whead. I am for you, Sir.   [Wheadle *and the* Second *feem to fight.*

Cul. Hold, hold, I befeech you, Mr. *Palmer,* hear me,
Hear me.

Whead. What's the matter?

Cul.

Cul. My Conscience will not let me fight in a wrong
Cause; I will pay the money, I have fairly lost it.

Whead. How contemptible is man, overcome by the worst of
Passions, Fear! it makes him as much below Beasts
As Reason raises him above them. I will my self
Fight you both; Come on, if you dare. ——

Cul. Prethee, dear *Wheadle*, do but hear me.

Whead. I disown all the kindness I ever had for you :
VVhere are these men of valour, which owe their
Virtue to this Mans Vice? let me go, I will chastise
Their insolence my self. 　　　　　　　　　　[*Cully holds him.*

Cul. Dear *Wheadle*, bear with the frailties of
Thy Friend.

Whead. Death, what wou'd you have me do? Can I serve
You with any thing more dear than my Life?

Cul. Let us give them security.

Whead. Do you know what it is you wou'd do? have you consider'd
VVhat a thousand Pounds is? 'tis a Fortune for any one Man.

Cul. I will pay it all, thou shalt be no loser.

Whead. Do you hear, Shepherd? how do you expect
This money?

Palm. I expect such security for it as my Friend shall advise.

Sec. A VVarrant to confess a Judgment from you both.

Whead. You shall be damn'd first; you shall
Have nothing.

Palm. and Sec. VVe'll have your bloods.
　　　　　　　　　[*They proffer to fight ; Cully holds* VVheadle.

Whead. Let me go.

Cul. Dear *Wheadle*, let it be so. You shall
Have a Judgment, Gentlemen.

Whead. I will take care hereafter with whom I engage.
　　　　　　　　　[*The Second pulls Papers out of his pocket.*
VVhat? you have your tacklings about you.

Sec. VVe have Articles for Peace, as well as VVeapons
For VVar.

Whead. Dispatch, dispatch them, put me to no more
Torment with delays.

Sec. Come Sir *Nicholas* to the Book; you see we are favourable,
VVe grant you the benefit of your Clergy　Your [*Cul. subscribes on* Palmer's
Helping hand, good Mr. *Wheadle*, to finish the work. *back and then* VVheadle.

VVhead. Take that into the bargain. 　　　　　　[*Kicks him.*

Palm. You shall have another, if you please, at the price.

Sec. VVe seldom quarrel under a thousand pounds.

Palm. and Sec. VVe wish you merry, Gentlemen.

　　　　　　　　　　　　　　　　　　　　　Palmer.

Palmer *sings.*

Come, let's to the Tavern scape,
And drink whilst we can stand;
We thirst more for the blood o' th' Grape
Than for the blood of man.

[*Exeunt* Palmer *and* Second.

Whead. Do you see now what men of mighty prowess
These are?
Cul. I was too blame indeed.
Whead. I am in such a passion I know not what
To do: Let us not stand gazing here;
I wou'd not have this known for a Kingdom.
Cul. No, nor I neither.
[*Exeunt.*

SCENE VI.

Scene, The Lord *Bevil's* House.

Enter my Lord Bevil *and* Lovis.

Lovis. 'Tis yet within your pow'r, Sir, to maintain
Our Honour, and prevent this threatning stain.
L. Bev. Forbear this wicked insolence: Once more
I charge you think on your Obedience. [*Exit* L. Bevil.
Lovis. Beauty, what art thou, we so much admire!
Thou art no real, but a seeming fire,
Which, like the glow-worm, only casts a light
To them whose Reason Passion does benight.
Thou art a Meteor, which but blazing dies,
Made of such Vapours as from us arise.
Within thy guilty beams lurk cruel Fates,
To peaceful Families, and warring States.
Unhappy Friend, to doat on what we know —— [*Ent. a Servant.*
Serv. Sir, Colonel *Bruce,* unexpectedly released from
His Imprisonment, is come to wait upon you. [*Exit Servant.*
Lovis. What shall I do! Ye Powers above be kind,
Some counsel give to my distracted mind:
Friendship and shame within me so contend,
I know not how to shun or meet my Friend.
Enter Bruce.
Bruce. Where is my gen'rous Friend? Oh noble Youth,
How long have I been rob'd of this content? [*They Embrace.*
Though deprivation be the greatest pain.

When

When Heav'n reftores our Happinefs again,
It makes amends by our Encreafe of Joy,
Perfecting that which it did once deftroy.
Dear Friend, my Love does now exact its Due ;
Graciana muft divide my Heart with you :
Conduct me to your Sifter, where I may
Make this my Morn of Joy a glorious Day.
What means this fad Aftonifhment !

   Lovis. How can we chufe but with Confufion greet,
When I your Joys with equal Sorrows meet.

   Bruce. O Heav'n ! Muft my Afflictions have no End !
I fcap'd my Foe to perifh by my Friend :
What ftrange Difafter can produce this Grief !
Is *Graciana* dead ? Speak, fpeak: Be brief.

   Lovis. She lives ; but I could wifh her dead.

   Bruce. Rafh Man ! Why fhould your Envy fwell fo high,
To wifh the World this great Calamity ?
Wifh the whole Frame of Nature were diffolv'd ;
That all things to a Chaos were revolv'd.
There is more Charity in this Defire ;
Since with our Lofs, our Sorrows wou'd expire.

              Enter Aurelia.

   Lovis Here comes *Aurelia*, fent for my Relief :
Heav'n knows her Tongue can beft exprefs this Grief :
Examine her, and you fhall find ere long,
I can avenge, though not relate your Wrong.

   Bruce. For pity, hafte *Aurelia*, and declare   [*Kiffes her Hand.*
The Reafons of your Brother's frighting Care :
My Soul is rack'd with Doubts, until I know.   [*After a paufe.*
Your Silence and your Looks. *Aurelia,* fhow
As if your Kindnefs made you bear a Part
Of thofe great Sorrows that afflict his Heart.

   Aurel. His Paffion is fo Noble and fo Juft,
No gen'rous Soul can know it but it muft
Lay claim unto a Portion, as its Due ;
He can be thus concern'd for none but you.

   Bruce. Kind Maid, reveal what my Misfortunes are ;
Friendfhip muft not engrofs them, though it fhare.
I wou'd not willingly my Love fufpect ;
And yet, I fear, 'tis anfwer'd with Neglect.

   Aurel. My Sifter, by unlucky Stars mif-led,
From you, and from her Happinefs is fled ;
Unskilful in the Way, by Paffion preft,
She has took Shelter in another's Breft.

            F   *Bruce.*

Bruce. Fate thou haft done thy worft, Thy Triumph fing ;
Now thou haft ftung fo home, th'aft loft thy Sting.
I have not Power *Graciana* to exclaim   *[After a paufe.*
Againft your Fault ; indeed you are to blame.

   Lovis. Tell me, did fhe her Promife plight, or give
Your Love encouragement enough to live ?

   Bruce. It was her pity fure, and not her Love,
That made her feem my Paffion to approve :
My Story was unpleafant to her Ear
At firft ; but time had made her apt to hear
My Love : fhe told me that it grew her Grief,
As much as mine, my Pain found no Relief ;
Then promis'd fhe'd endeavour the decreafe
Of that in her which warr'd againft my Peace,
'Twas in this joyful Spring of Love that I
Was ravifh'd from her by our Enemy :
My Hopes grew ftrong, I banifh'd all Defpair :
Thefe glowing Sparks I then left to the Care
Of this fair Maid, thinking fhe might infpire
My Paffion, and blow up the kindling Fire.

   Lovis. Alas ; She to my knowledge has been true ;
Sh'a fpoke and figh'd all that fhe cou'd for you.

   Aurel. When you were forc'd to end, I did proceed,
And with Succefs the catching Fire did feed :
Till Noble *Beaufort*, one unlucky Day,
A Vifit to our Family did pay ;
Newly arriv'd from Foreign Courts, and fraught
With all thofe Virtues that in Courts are taught :
He with his am'rous Tales fo charm'd her Ear,
That fhe of Love from none but him wou'd hear.

   Bruce. That Heart, which I fo long with Toil and Pain
Befieg'd, and us'd all Stratagems to gain,   *[Enter a Servant and*
Is now become, within a trice, we fee,   *whifpers with* Lovis,
The Triumph of another's Victory.
There is a Fate in Love, as well as War ;
Some, though lefs careful, more fuccefsful are.

   Lovis. Do not this Opportunity withftand ;
Thefe Lovers now are walking Hand in Hand
I'th' Garden ; fight him there, and facrifice
His Heart to that falfe Woman's Cruelties :
If Fate be fo unjuft to make thee fall,
His Blood or mine fhall wait thy *Funeral.*

   Bruce. Young Man, this Rafhnefs muft have my Excufe,
Since 'tis your *Friendfhip* does your *Fault* produce ;

                                     If

Powers above did not this Paffion fway,
But that our Love our Reafon did obey,
Your Sifter I with juftice might accufe,
Nor wou'd I this Occafion then refufe.

 Lovis. Does *Bruce* refolve thus tamely to decline
His Int'reft, and like foolifh Women pine?
Can that great Heart which in your Breaft does dwell,
Let your fond Griefs above your Courage fwell?

 Bruce. My Paffions grow unruly, and I find
Too foon, they'll raife a Tempeft in my mind.
Graciana, like fond Parents, y'are to blame,
You did not in its Youth correct my Flame;
'Tis now fo head-ftrong, and fo wild a Fire,
I fear to both our Ruines 'twill confpire:
I grow impatient, Friend, come lead me where
I may to her my injur'd Love declare.
Graciana, yet your Heart fhall be my Prize,
Or elfe my Heart fhall be your Sacrifice.
Defpair's the Iffue of ignoble Minds,
And but with Cowards Entertainment finds. [*Exeunt* Lovis *and* Bruce.

 Aurel. Heav'n grant fome Moderation to this Rage,
That Reafon their fwell'd Paffions may affwage.
Oh *Bruce!* thou little think'ft the Fates in me
Have to the full reveng'd thy Injury.   [*Exit.*

SCENE VII.

Scene, a Garden belonging to my Lord *Bevil's* Houfe.

Enter Beaufort *and* Graciana.

 Beauf. Madam, what you have told, fo much muft move
All that have fenfe of Honour or of Love,
That for my Rival I cou'd fhed a Tear,
If Grief had any power when you are near.

 Grac. Leave this Difcourfe; your Miftrefs you neglect,
And to your Rival all your Thoughts direct.

    Enter Bruce *and* Lovis, *and ftand undifcovered.*

 Beauf. Forgive me, dear *Graciana,* I have been
By my compaffion footh'd into a fin.
The holieft Man that to the Altar bows
With wandring Thoughts too often ftains his Vows.

 Bruce. Graciana, you are alter'd much, I find; [*Surprifing her by the hand.*
Since I was here y' have learn'd how to be kind.
The God of Love, which fubt'ly let you fway,

               Has

Has ftoln your Heart, and taught it to obey.

   Grac. Heav'ns ! what ftrange furprife is this !

   Bruc. Hither I'm come to make my lawful claim ;
You are my Miftrefs, and muft own my Flame.

   Beauf. Forbear, bold Man, and do not tempt thy Fate ; [*Taking her by the*
Thou haft no Right, her Love does Right create :   *other hand.*
Thy Claim muft to my Title here give place ;
'Tis not who loves, but whom fhe's pleas'd to grace.

   Grac. Hear me but fpeak ; *Bruce,* you divide my Care,
Though not my Love, you my Compaffion fhare ;
My Heart does double Duty ; it does mourn
For you brave *Bruce* ; for you brave *Beaufort* burn.

   Bruce. Your pity but deftroys : if you wou'd fave,
It is your Love, *Graciana,* I muft have.

   Beauf. Her Love is mine, fhe did it now declare ;
Name it no more, but vanifh and defpair.

   Bruce. Death, do you think to conjure me away !
I am no Devil that am forc'd t'obey :
If y'are fo good at that, here are fuch Charms [*Laying his hand on his Sword*
Can fright y'into the Circle of her Arms.

   Beauf. Here is a Sword more fit for my Defence ;
This is not Courage, *Bruce,* but Infolence. [*Grac. takes Beauf. in her arms.*
Graciana, let me go, my Heart wants room.

   Grac. My Arms till now were ne're thought troublefome.

   Bruce. *Beaufort,* I hope y'have Courage to appear,
VVhere facred Sanctuary is not near.
I'll leave you now within that happy ftate
VVhich does provoke my Fury and my Hate.   [*Ex. Bru. and* Lov.

   Grac. You muft not meet him in the Field, to prove
A doubtful Combat, for my certain Love.
Befide, your Heart is mine ; will you expofe
The Heart you gave me, to its raging Foes ?
Thofe Men want Honour who ftake that at Play
VVhich to their Friends their Kindnefs gave away.

   Beauf. *Gratiana,* why did you confine me fo,
Within your Arms ? you fhou'd have let me go :
We foon had finifht this our hot debate,
Which now muft wait a longer time on Fate.

   Grac. None in Combuftions blame fuch as defire
To fave their precious Goods from raging Fire.
Banifh this Paffion now, my Lord, and prove
Your Anger cannot over-cloud your Love.

   Beauf. Your glorious Prefence can this Rage controul,
And make a Calm in my tempeftuous Soul ;

                                 But

But yet there muſt be time; the Sun does bear
A while with the fierce Tempeſts of the Air,
Before he make thoſe ſtormy Conflicts ceaſe,
And with his conquering Beams proclaims a Peace.   [*Exeunt.*

ACT IV. SCENE I.

Enter Lord Beaufort *and* Lovis.

Lovis. FArewel, my Lord, I'll to my Friend declare
How gen'rous you in your Acceptance were.
Beauf. My Honour is as forward as my Love,
On equal Wings of Jealouſie they move:
I to my Rival will in neither yield;
I've won the Chamber, and will win the Field.
Lovis. Your Emulation, Sir, is ſwoln ſo high,
You may be worthy of his Victory:
You'll meet with Honour blown, not in the Bud,
Whoſe Root was fed with vaſt expence of Blood.   [*Exit* Lovis.

Enter Sir Frederick.

Sir Fred. What, my Lord, as ſtudious as a Country Vicar
On a Saturday in the Afternoon?
I thought you had been ready for the Pulpit.
Beauf. I am not ſtudying Speeches for my Miſtreſs;
'Tis Action that I now am thinking on;
Wherein there's Honour to be gain'd;
And you, Couſin, are come luckily to ſhare it.
Sir Fred. On my Life, a Prize to be plaid for your Miſtreſs:
I had notice of your Quarrel, which brought me hither
So early with my Sword to ſerve you.
But dares ſo zealous a Lover as your Lordſhip
Break the Commandment of your Miſtreſs?
I heard, poor Lady, ſhe wept, and charg'd you
To ſleep in a whole Skin; but young Men
Never know when th' are well.
Beauf. Couſin, my Love to her cannot make me forget
My Duty to my Family.
Sir Fred. Pray whoſe Body muſt I exerciſe my Skill upon?
Beauf. You met the Man; *Graciana's* Brother.
Sir Fred. An expert Gentleman, and I have not fenc'd of late,
Unleſs it were with my

Widow's

Widow's Maids; and they are e'en too hard for me,
At my own Weapon.

Beauf. Cofin, 'tis time we were preparing for the Field

Sir Fred. I wait to ferve you, Sir.

Beauf. But yet with Grief, *Graciana*, I muft go,
Since I your Brother there fhall meet my Foe :
My Fate too near refembles theirs where he
Did wound himfelf that hurt his Enemy.   [*Exeunt.*

SCENE II.

Enter Wheadle, *and* Palmer *drefs'd like the Lord* Bevil.

Whead. So, my *Proteus*, exactly drefs'd !
Dexterous Rogue ! is *Grace* ready in her Geers,
And fettl'd in my Lady *Dauwbwell*'s Houfe ?

Palm. Every Trap is baited.

Whead. I'll warrant you then we catch our *Cully :*
He's gone to put himfelf into a fantafttick Garb,
In Imitation of Sir *Frederick Frolick* ;
He's almoft frantick with the very conceit
Of gaining the rich Widow.   But hark,
I hear him coming ; flip down the back way,
And to your charge.   [*Exit* Palmer.

Enter Cully.

Sir Nich. *Wheadle*, and what think you of this Habit ?
Is it not very modifh ?

Whead. As any Man need wear :
How did you furnifh your felf fo fuddenly ?

Sir Nich. Suddenly ? I proteft, I was, at leaft,
At Sixteen Broaker's, before I could put my felf
Exactly into the Fafhion ; but now I defie Sir *Frederick* ;
I am as fine as he, and I will be as mad as he,
If that will carry the Widow,
I'll warrant thee.

Whead. Is it not better pufhing thus for a Fortune,
Before your Reputation's blafted
VVith the infamous Names of Coward and Gamefter ?
And fo become able to pay the Thoufand Pounds without noife,
Than going into the Country, felling your Land,
Making a Havock among your VVoods, or mortgaging
Your Eftate to a fcrupulous Scrivener, that will
VVhifper it into the Ears of the whole Town,

By.

By inquiring of your good Behaviour?

Sir *Nich.* Excellent *Wheadle!* And will my Lord
Bevil speak my Commendations to his
Sister?

Whead. She is impatient till she see you, Sir;
For in my hearing, upon the Account I gave him
Of you, he told her you were the prettiest, wittiest,
Wildest Gentleman about the Town, and a Cavalier
In your Heart; the only things that take her.

Sir *Nich. Wheadle,* Come, I will go to the Tavern,
And swallow two whole Quarts of Wine
Instantly, and, when I am drunk,
Ride on a Drawer's Back to visit her.

Whead. Some less Frollick to begin with.

Sir *Nich.* I will cut three Drawers over the Pate then,
And go with a Tavern-Lanthorn before me at Noon-Day.
Come away.   [*Exeunt,* Cully *singing.*

SCENE III.

Enter Palmer *and* Grace.

Palm. Do not I look like a very Reverend Lord,
Grace?

Grace. And I like a very fine Lady, Mr. *Palmer?*

Palm. Yes in good Faith, *Grace;* what a rogue is that
Wheadle, to have kept such a Treasure to himself.
Without communicating a little to his Friends?   [*Offers to kiss her.*

Grace. Forbear; you'l be out in your Part,
My Lord, when Sir *Nicholas* comes.

Palm. The truth is, my Lady, I am better
Prepar'd at this time to act a Lover,
Than a Relation.

Grace. That grave Dress is very amorous indeed.

Palm. My Vertues, like those of Plants in the Winter,
Are retired; your warm Spring
Wou'd fetch 'em out with a Vengeance.

Enter Jenny *in haste.*

Jenny. Mr. *Wheadle* and Sir *Nich'las* are come.

Palm. Away, away then, Sister, expect your Kew.

Enter Wheadle *and Sir* Nicholas, *kicking a Tavern-Boy before him who has Three Bottles of Wine on a Rope hanging at his Back.*

Cul. singing. *Then march along, Boys; valiant and strong Boys.*
So lay down the Bottles here.

                                        Whead.

Whead. My Lord, this is the worthy Gentleman
That I told you was
Ambitious to be your Sister's Servant.

   Cul. Hither am I come, my Lord, to drink
Your Sister's Health, without Offence, I hope.

   Palm. You are heartily welcome, Sir.

   Cul. Here's a Brimmer then to her, and all the
Fleas about her.

   Palm. Sir, I'll call her to pledge it.

   Cul. Stay, stay, my Lord, that you may
Be able to tell her you have drunk it.   [*Palmer drinks and exit.*
Wheadle, How do you like this?   [*Draws his Sword.*
Shall I break the Windows?

   Whead. Hold, Hold;
You are not in a House of evil Reputation.

   Cul. Well admonish'd, Sir *Fredrick Frollick.*
                   Enter Palmer *and* Grace.

   Palm, This is Sir *Nich'las,* Sister.

   Cul. I, Madam, I am Sir *Nich'las,* and how do you like me?

   Grace. A pretty Gentleman.
Pray, Sir, are you come a House-warming,
That you bring Wine with you?

   Cul. If you ask such pert Questions,   [*Kisses her.*
Madam, I can stop your Mouth.
Hither am I come to be drunk,
That you may see me drunk; and
Here's a Health to your Flannel Petticoat.   [*Drinks.*

   Grace. Mr. *Wheadle,* my Service to you; a Health
To Sir *Nich'las*'s great Grand-Father's Beard-Brush. [*She drinks part.*

   Cul. Nay, pledge me; Ha———

   Grace. You are not quarrelsome in your Drink,
I hope, Sir.

   Cul. No, faith; I am wond'rous loving.   [*Hugs her.*

   Grace. You are a very bold Lover.

   Cul. Widow, let you and I go upon the Ramble
To Night.

   Grace. Do you take me for a Night-walker, Sir?

   Cul. Thou shalt be Witness how many Constables
Staves I'll break about the Watch-Mens Ears:
How many Bell Men I'll rob of their Verses,
To furnish a little Apartment in the Back-side
Of my Lodging.

   Grace. I believe y' are an excellent Man at
Quarter staff, Sir.

                                      Cul.

Cul. The odds was on my head againſt any Warrener
In all our Country ; But I have left it off this
Two year. My Lord, what ſay you, Do you think
Your Siſter and I ſhou'd not furniſh a Bed-chamber
As well as two ſoberer people ? what think you, my Lord ?

Grace. I, and a Nurſery too, I hope, Sir.

Cul. Well ſaid, Widow, i'faith ; I will get upon thy body
A generation of wild Cats, children that ſhall
Waw, waw, ſcratch their Nurſes, and be drunk
With their Sucking-bottles.

Whead. Brave Sir *Nich'las.*

Cul. *Wheadle,* give me a Brimmer ; the Widow
Shall drink it to our Progeny.
Where, where is ſhe gone ?   [*Exit* Grace.

Palm. You have frighted her hence, Sir.

Cul. I'll fright her worſe, if I find her in a Corner.
Ha, Widow, I'll follow you ; I'll follow you, ha.   [*Exit* Culley.

Whead. The Wine makes the Rogue witty ; he
Over-acts the Part I gave him ;
Sir *Frederick* is not half ſo mad : I will keep
Him thus elevated till he has married *Grace,*
And we have the beſt part of his eſtate at our mercy.

Palm. Moſt ingenious *Wheadle !*

Whead. I was not born to eaſe nor Acres ;
Induſtry is all my ſtock of living.   [*The women ſhriek within.*

Palm. Hark, he puts them to the ſqueek.

Whead. We muſt go and take him off ; he's as fierce
As a Bandog that has newly broke his chain.   [*Exeunt laughing.*

SCENE IV.

Scene, A Field.

Enter Bruce *and* Lovis, *and traverſe the Stage.*

Then enter four or five men in diſguiſes.

1 *Man.* This way they went ; be ſure you kill the Villain :
Let pity be a ſtranger to your breaſts.

2 *Man.* We have been bred, you know, unacquainted with
Compaſſion.

3 *Man.* But why, Colonel, ſhou'd you ſo eagerly
Purſue his Life ? he has the report of
A gallant Man.

1 *Man.* He murdered my Father.

G   3 *Man*

3 *Man.* I have heard he kill'd him fairly in
The Field at *Nasby.*

1 *Man.* He kill'd him, that's enough; and I my self
Was witness; I accus'd him to the
Protector, and suborn'd Witness
To have taken away his Life by form
Of Law; but my Plot was discover'd, and
He yesterday releas'd; since which I've
Watch'd an opportunity, without the
Help of seeming Justice, for my Revenge.
Strike home. ——

3 *Man.* We are your hired slaves; and since
You'l have it so, we'll shed his blood,
And never spare our own.   [*Exeunt, drawing their Swords.*

Enter Beaufort *and* Sir Frederick, *and traverse the Stage.*
Enter Bruce *and* Lovis *at another door.*

Bruce. Your Friendship, noble Youth, 's too prodigal;
For one already lost you venture all;
Your present happiness, your future joy;
You for the hopeless your great hopes destroy.

Lovis. What can I venture for so brave a friend?
I have no hopes but what on you depend.
Shou'd I your Friendship and my Honour rate
Below the value of a poor Estate,
A heap of dirt! Our Family has been
To blame, my blood must here atone the sin.

Enter the five *Villains with drawn Swords.*

Heav'ns! what is there an Ambuscado laid!
Draw, dearest Friend, I fear we are betray'd.

1 *Vil. Bruce,* look on me and then prepare to die.   [*Pulling off his*
Bruce. O Treacherous Villain!   *Vizard.*
1 *Vil.* Fall on, and sacrifice his blood to my Revenge.
Lovis. More hearts than one shall bleed if he must die.   [*They fight.*

Enter Beaufort *and* Sir Frederick.

Beauf. Heavens! what's this I see! Sir *Frederick,* draw;
Their blood's too good to grace such
Villains Swords. Courage, brave men; now
VVe can match their Force.

Lovis. VVe'l make you, slaves, repent   [*The Villains run.*
This Treachery.

Beauf. So.

Bruce. They are not worth pursuit; we'll let them go.
Brave men! this action makes it well appear

'Tis

'Tis Honour and not Envy brings you here.

Beauf. VVe come to conquer, *Bruce*, and not to fee
Such Villains rob us of our Victory.
Your Lives our fatal Swords claim as their due ;
VV'ad wrong'd our felves had we not righted you.

Bruce. Your gen'rous courage has oblig'd us fo,
That to your fuccour we our fafety owe.

Lovis. Y'ave done what men of Honour ought to do,
VVhat in your caufe we wou'd have done for you.

Beauf. You fpeak the truth, w'ave but our duty done ;
Prepare : Duty's no obligation.   [*He ftrips.*

Bruce. My Honour is dif-fatisfi'd; I muft, [*Lovis and Sir Frederick ftrip.*
My Lord, confider whether it be juft
To draw my Sword againft that Life which gave
Mine, but e'en now, protection from the grave.

Beauf. None come into the Field to weigh what's right,
This is no place for Counfel, but for Fight :
Difpatch.

Bruce. I am refolv'd I will not fight.

Beauf. Did I come hither then only to fright
A Company of fearful Slaves away ?
My Courage ftoops not at fo mean a prey :
Know, *Bruce*, I hither come to fhed thy blood.

Bruce. Open this bofom, and let out a flood.

Beauf. I come to conquer bravely in the Field,
Not to take poor revenge on fuch as yield.
Has nothing pow'r, too backward man, to move
Thy Courage ? Think on thy neglected Love :
Think on the beauteous *Graciana*'s Eyes ;
'Tis I have robb'd thee of that glorious prize.

Bruce. There are fuch charms in *Graciana*'s Name,   [*Strips haftily.*
My fcrup'lous Honour muft obey my Flame :
My lazy Courage I with fhame condemn :
No thoughts have power ftreams of blood to ftem.

Sir Fred. Come, Sir, out of kindnefs to our Friends,
You and I muft pafs a fmall complement
On each other.   [*They all fight.*

Beaufort *after many Paffes clofes with* Bruce ; *they fall ;* Beaufort
difarms him.

Beauf. Here, live.   [*Giving* Bruce *his Sword again.*

Bruce. My Lord, y'ave gain'd a perfect Victory ;
Y'ave vanquifh'd and oblig'd your Enemy.

Beauf. Hold, gallant men.

Bruce *and* Beaufort *part* Lovis *and* Sir Frederick.

G 2   *Lovis.*

Lovis. Before we bleed: Do we here fight a Prize,
Where handfom proffers may for Wounds fuffice?
I am amaz'd! what means this bloodlefs Field!

Bruce. The ftouteft heart muft to his fortune yield.
Brave Youth! here Honour did with Courage vie,   [*To* Beauf.
And both agree to grace your Victory.
Heaven with fuch a Conqueft favours few:
'Tis eafier to deftroy than to fubdue.
Our bodies may by brutifh force be kill'd;
But noble Minds alone to Virtue yield.
My Lord, I've twice receiv'd my Life from you;
Much is to both thofe gen'rous actions due;
The nobler giver I muft highly prize,
Though I the Gift, Heav'n knows, as much defpife.
Can I defire to live, when all the Joy
Of my poor Life its Ranfom does deftroy!
No, no, *Graciana*'s lofs I'll ne'r furvive:
I pay too dear for this unfought Reprieve.
      [*Falls on his Sword, and is defperately wounded.*

Beauf. Hold, gallant Man! Honour her felf does bleed;
      [*Running to him, takes him in his arms.*
All gen'rous hearts are wounded by this deed.

Lovis. He does his blood for a loft Miftrefs fpend;
And fhall not I bleed for fo brave a Friend?
      [*Lovis offers to fall on his Sword, but is hindered by*
        Sir *Frederick.*

Sir *Fred.* Forbear, Sir, the Frollick's not to go round, as I
Take it.

Beauf. 'Twere greater Friendfhip to affift me here:
I hope the wound's not mortal, though I fear ——

Bruce. My Sword, I doubt, has fail'd in my relief;
'T has made a vent for blood, but not for grief.
      [Bruce *frugling,* Lovis *and* Sir Frederick *help to hold him.*
Let me once more the unkind Weapon try:
VVill ye prolong my pain? oh cruelty!

Lovis. Ah deareft *Bruce,* can you thus carelefs be
Of our great Friendfhip, and your Loyalty!
Look on your Friend; your drooping Country view;
And think how much they both expect from you.
You for a Miftrefs wafte that precious blood,
VVhich fhou'd be fpent but for our Mafters good.

Sir *Fred.* Expence of blood already makes him faint;
Let's carry him to the next Houfe, till we can
Procure a Chair to convey him to my Lord *Bevil's,*

                          The

The beſt place for accommodation.   [*They all take him up.*

  Beauf. Honour has plaid an after-game ; this Field
The Conq'rour does unto the Conquer'd yield.   [*Exeunt.*

SCENE V.

Enter Graciana *weeping.*

  Grac. Farewel all thoughts of happineſs, farewel :
My Fears together with my Sorrows ſwell :
VVhilſt from my Eyes there flows this Cryſtal Flood,
From their brave hearts there flows ſuch ſtreams of Blood.
Here I am loſt, while both for me contend ;
VVith what ſucceſs can this ſtrange Combate end !
Honour with Honour fights for Victory,
And Love is made the common Enemy.
                Enter Lord Bevil.
  L. Bevil. VVeeping ! Ah Child ! ——.
  Grac. Kill me not with expectation, Sir.
  L. Bev. The gen'rous *Bruce* has kill'd himſelf
For you : Being diſarm'd, and at his Rival's mercy,
His Life and Sword were given him by the
Noble Youth ; He made a brave acknowledgment
For both ; but then confidering you were loſt,
He ſcorn'd to live ; and falling on his Sword,
Has giv'n himſelf a mortal wound.   [*Exit L.* Bevil.
                Enter Aurelia *weeping.*
  Aurel. Cruel *Graciana*, Go but in and ſee
The fatal Triumph of your Victory.
The Noble *Bruce*, to your eternal ſhame,
VVith his own blood has quench'd his raging flame.
  Grac. Weeping. My carriage ſhall in theſe misfortunes prove
That I have Honour too, as well as Love.
  Aurel. aſide. Thy ſorrows, ſad *Aurelia*, will declare
At once, I fear, thy Love and thy Deſpair :
Theſe ſtreams of grief ſtraight to a flood will riſe ;
I can command my Tongue, but not my Eyes.   [*Exit* Aurel.
  Grac. In what a Maze, *Graciana*, doſt thou tread !
VVhich is the path that doth to Honour lead ?
I in this Lab'rinth ſo reſolve to move,
That none ſhall judge I am miſled by Love.
                Enter Beaufort.
  Beauf. Here Conq'rours muſt forget their Victories,
And homage pay to your Victorious Eyes.

                                  Graciana

Graciana, hither your poor Slave is come,
After his Conquest to receive his doom :
Smile on his Vict'ry ; had he prov'd untrue
To Honour, he had then prov'd false to you.

   Grac. Perfidious Man, can you expect from me
An approbation of your Treachery !
VVhen I, distracted with prophetick fears,
Blasted with sighs, and almost drown'd in tears,
Begg'd you to moderate your Rage last night,
Did you not promise me you wou'd not fight ?
Go now and triumph in your Victory ;
Into the Field you went my Enemy,
And are return'd the only Man I hate,
The wicked Instrument of my sad fate.
My Love has but dissembled been to thee
To try my gen'rous Lover's constancy.   [*Exit* Graciana,

   Beauf. Oh Heav'n ! how strange and cruel is my fate !
Preserv'd by Love, to be destroy'd by hate !   [*Exit* Beaufort.

SCENE VI.

Scene, The Widow's House.

    Enter Betty *and* Lettice, *the two Chamber-maids, severally.*
   Betty. Oh, *Lettice*, we have staid for you.

   Lett. VVhat hast thou done to the French-man,
Girl ? he lies yonder neither dead nor drunk ;
No body knows what to make of him.

   Betty. I sent for thee to help make sport with him ;
He'll come to himself, never fear him :
Have you not observ'd how scurvily h'as look'd
Of late ?

   Lett. Yes ; and he protests it is for love of you.

   Betty. Out upon him, for a dissembling Rascal ;
H's got the foul Disease ;
Our Coach man discover'd it by a Bottle of Diet
Drink he brought and hid behind the stairs, into which
I infus'd a little *Opium.*

   Lett. VVhat dost intend to do with him ?
   Betty. You shall see.

    *Enter Coach-man with a Tub without a bottom, a spout at the top to be
lock'd, and a hole to put ones head out at, made easie to be born on
ones shoulders.*

   Coach-m. Here's the Tub ; where's the French man ?

                                                    Betty

Betty. He lies behind the flairs ; hafte and bring him in,
That he may take quiet poffeffion of this wooden Tenement ;
For 'tis near his time of waking.

The Coach man and another Servant bring in Dufoy, *and put him into the Tub.*

Is the Fidler at hand that us'd to ply at the blind
Ale-houfe ?

Coach m. He's ready.

Enter a Fidler.

Betty. VVell, let's hear now what a horrible noife you
Can make to wake this Gentleman.　　　　　*[Fidler plays a Tune.*

Lett. He wants a helping hand ; his Eye-lids　*[*Dufoy *begins to wake.*
Are feal'd up; fee how the wax fticks upon 'em.
Let me help you, Monfieur.

Dufoy. Vat aré you? Jarnie! vat is dis! am I
Jack in a boxe? begar, who did putté
Me here ?

Betty. Good-morrow, Monfieur ; will you be pleas'd
To take your Pills this Morning ?

Dufoy. Noé : but I vo'd have de diable take youé ;
It vas youé dat did abufé me dus, vas
It noté? begar I vil killé ale de
Shamber-maid in *Englandé.*

Lett. VVill you be pleas'd to drink, Monfieur ?
There's a Bottle of your Diet-drink within.

Dufoy. Are youé de littel diable come to tormenté mé ?
Morbleu ! vas ever man afronté in dis naturé !

Betty. Me-thinks he has ferbon, mine Monfieur,
Now if you pleafe to make your little Addreffé,
And your amouré, you will not find me fo coy.

Dufoy. Begar I vil no marié de coufin Germain
Of de diable.

Lett. What fhou'd he do with a Wife? he has not
Houfe room for her.

Betty. VVhy do you not keep your head within
Doors, Monfieur ?

Lett. Now there's fuch a ftorm abroad.

Dufoy. Why did not youé keep your Maiden-headé
Vid in dooré? begar, tellé me daté.

Coach-m. Have you any fine French Commodities to fell,
Gloves and Ribbands? y'ave got
A very convenient Shop, Monfieur.

Dufoy. I do hope you vil have verié
Convenient halteré, begar.

Jerny

Jerny, Can I not taré dis tingé in de pieces?

Betty. You begin to fweat, Monſieur; the Tub is
Proper for you.

Dufoy. I have no more patiencé;
I vil breaké dis priſon, or I vil breaké
My neké, and ye ſhall alé be hangé.   [*Struggles to get out.*

Lett. He begins to rave; bleſs the poor Man.

Betty. Some Muſick quickly, to
Compoſe his mind.   [*The Muſick plays; and they Dance about him.*
How prettily the Snail carries his Tenement   [*He walks with the Tub on his*
On his back! I'm ſorry I am but his Miſtreſs: *back.*
If I had been your VVife, Monſieur, I had made
You a compleat Snail; your Horns
Shou'd have appear'd.

Dufoy. I vil have de patiencé, dere is no oder remedé;
You be alé de Raskalé VVhore; de diable
Take you alé; and I vil ſay no more, begar.

Betty. This is a very fine Veſſel, and wou'd ſwim well;
Let's to the Horſe pond with him.

Lett. Come, come, he looks as ſullenly as a Hare
In her Form; let's leave him.

Coach-m. Your Serviteur tres humble, Monſieur. [*Exeunt all but* Dufoy.

Dufoy. Bougre, I canno hangé my ſelfé; begar I canno
Drowné my ſelfé; I vil go hidé my ſelfé,
And ſtarvé to dyé; I vil no be de laughé
For every Jackanapé Engliſhé. Morbleu.

SCENE VII.

Sir Frederick *is brought in upon a Bier, with a mourning Cloth over him, at-*
tended by a Gentleman in a mourning Cloak: Four Fidlers carry the Corps,
with their Inſtruments tuck'd under their Cloaks.

Enter the Widow weeping.

Mourner. Madam, you muſt expect a bloody conſequence
VVhen men of ſuch prodigious Courage fight.
The young Lord *Beaufort* was the firſt that fell,
After his Sword too deeply had engag'd
His Rival not to ſtay behind him long.
Sir *Frederick* with your Nephew bravely fought;
Death long did keep his diſtance, as if he
Had fear'd exceſs of Valour; but when they,
Ore-loaded with their wounds, began to faint,
He with his terrors did invade their Breaſts.

Fame

Fame foon brought many to the Tragick Place,
Where I found my deareft Friend, Sir *Frederick,*
Almoft as poor in *Breath* as *Blood:*
He took me by the Hand, and all the Stock h'ad left
He fpent, Madam, in calling upon you.
He firft proclaim'd your Vertues, then his Love;
And having charg'd me to convey his Corpfe hither,
To wait on you, his lateft *Breath* expir'd
With the Command.

 Wid. The VVorld's too poor to recompenfe this Lofs.
Unhappy VVoman! why fhou'd I furvive
The only Man in whom my Joys did live?
My dreadful Grief!   *[The Fidlers prepare.*

    Enter Dufoy *in his Tub.*
 Dufoy. Oh my Matré, my Matré! who has kill my
Matré? Morbleu, I vil——   *[The Widow fhrieks, and runs out: All the*
            Fidlers run out in a Fright.
Oh, de Diablé, de Diablé! *[Sir* Frederick *ftarts up, which frights* Dufoy.
 Sir Fred. VVhat Devillifh Accident is this?
Or has the VVidow undermin'd me?
      [Enter the VVidow *and her Maid, laughing.*
I fhall be laugh'd to Death now indeed,
By Chamber-Maids; why have you no
Pity, VVidow?
 Wid. None at all for the Living; Ha, ha, ha.
You fee w'are provided for your Frollicks, Sir; Ha, ha.
 Sir Fred. Laugh but one Minute longer, I will forfwear
Thy Company, kill thy Tabby Cat, and make thee weep
For ever after.
 Wid. Farewel, Sir, expect at night to fee the old Man,
VVith his Paper Lanthorn, and crack'd Spectacles,
Singing your woful Tragedy
To Kitchin-Maids, and Coblers Prentices.
    [Widow offers to go, Sir Frederick *holds her by the Arm.*
 Sir Fred. Hark you, hark you, VVidow:
By all thofe Devils that have
Hitherto poffefs'd thy Sex——
 Wid. No Swearing, good Sir *Frederick.*
 Sir Fred. Set thy Face then; let me not fee the Remains
Of one poor Smile: So now I will kifs thee,
And be Friends.   *[Widow falls out a laughing.*
Not all thy Wealth fhall hire me to
Come within fmell of thy Breath again.
Jealoufie, and, which will be worfe for thee, Widow, Impotence
       H   Light

Light upon me, if I stay one Moment longer with thee.   [Offers to go.

Wid. Do you hear, Sir? Can you be so angry with one
That loves you so passionately she cannot survive
You?

Sir *Fred.* Widow, may the Desire of Man keep thee.
Waking, till thou art as mad as I am,   [*Exit Sir* Frederick.

Wid. How lucky was this Accident!
How he wou'd have insulted
Over my Weakness else!
Sir *Fred'rick,* since I've Warning, you shall prove
More subtil Ways, before I own my *Love.*   [Exeunt.

ACT V. SCENE I.

Scene, The Lord Bevil's *House.*

Enter Lovis, *a* Chirurgeon, *Servants, carrying* Bruce *in a Chair.*

Chir. COurage, brave Sir; do not mistrust my Art.

Bruce. Tell me, didst thou e'er cure a wounded Heart?
Thy Skill, fond Man, thou here imploy'st in vain;
The Ease thou giv'st does but encrease my Pain.

Lovis. Dear *Bruce,* my Life does on your Life depend;
Though you disdain to live, yet save your Friend.

Bruce. Do what you please; but are not those unkind
That ease the Body to afflict the Mind?   [*The* Chirurgeon *dresses him.*
Oh cruel Love! thou shoot'st with such strange Skill,
The Wounds thou mak'st will neither heal nor kill:
Thy flaming Arrows kindle such a Fire
As will not waste thy Victims, nor expire!
                    Enter Aurelia.

Lovis. Is the Wound mortal? Tell me,   [*To the* Chirurgeon.
Or may we cherish Hopes of his Recovery?

Chir. The Danger is not imminent: yet my Prognostick
Boads a sad Event: For though there be no great
Vessel dissected, yet I have cause to fear
That the *Parenchyma* of the right Lobe of the Lungs,
Near some large Branch of the *Aspera Arteria,*
Is perforated.

Lovis. Tell me in English, will he live or die?

Chir. Truly I despair of his Recovery.   [*Ex.* Chirurgeon.

Aurel. aside.] Forgive me, Ladies, if Excess of Love
Me beyond Rules of Modesty does move,

                                        And

And againſt Cuſtom, makes me now reveal
Thoſe Flames my tortur'd Breaſt did long conceal;
'Tis ſome Excuſe that I my Love declare
When there's no Med'cine left to cure Deſpair.   [Weeps by the Chair ſide.

   Bruce. Oh Heav'n; can fair *Aurelia* weep for me!
This is ſome Comfort to my Miſery.
Kind Maid, thoſe Eyes ſhould only Pity take
Of ſuch as feel no Wounds but what they make:
Who for another in your ſight does mourn,
Deſerves not your Compaſſion, but your Scorn.

   Aurel. I come not here with Tears to pity you;
I for your Pity with this Paſſion ſue.

   Bruce. My Pity! tell me what can be the Grief,
That from the Miſerable hopes Relief!

   Aurel. Before you know this Grief, you feel the Pain.

   Bruce. You cannot love, and not be lov'd again:
Where ſo much Beauty does with Love conſpire,
No Mortal can reſiſt that double Fire.

   Aurel. When proud *Graciana* wounded your brave Heart,
On poor *Aurelia's* you reveng'd the ſmart:
Whilſt you in vain did ſeek thoſe Wounds to cure,
With Patience, I their Torture did endure.

   Bruce. My Happineſs has been ſo long conceal'd,
That it becomes my Miſery reveal'd:
That which ſhould prove my Joy, now proves my Grief;
And that brings Pain, which known, had brought Relief.
Aurelia, why would you not let me know,
Whilſt I had power to pay the Debt I owe?
'Tis now too late; yet all I can I'll do,
I'll ſigh away the Breath I've left, for you.

   Aurel. You yet have power to grant me all I crave,
'Tis not your Love I court, I court your Grave.
I with my Flame ſeek not to warm your Breaſt,
But beg my Aſhes in your Urn may Reſt,
For ſince *Graciana's* Loſs you ſcorn'd t'out-live,
I am reſolv'd I'll not your Death ſurvive.

   Bruce. Hold, you too gen'rous are; yet I may live:
Heav'n for your ſake may grant me a Reprieve.

   Aurel. Oh, no! Heav'n has decreed, alas! that we
Shou'd in our Fates not in our Loves agree.

   Bruce. Dear Friend my Raſhneſs I too late repent;   [To Lovis.
I ne're thought Death till now a Puniſhment.
                Enter Graciana.

   Grac. Oh, do not talk of Death! that very Sound

                                           Once

Once more will give my Heart a mortal Wound:
Here on my Knees I've sinn'd I must confess
Against your Love, and my own Happiness;
I, like the Child, whose Folly proves his Loss,
Refus'd the Gold, and did accept the Dross.

  Bruce. You have in *Beaufort* made so good a choice,
His Virtue's such he has his Rival's Voice;
Graciana, none but his great Soul cou'd prove
VVorthy to be the Centre of your Love.

  Grac. Yon to another would such Virtue give,
Brave Sir, as in your self does only live.
If to the most deserving I am due,
He must resign his weaker Claim to you.

  Bruce. This is but Flatt'ry; for I'm sure you can
Think none so worthy as that gen'rous Man:
By Honour you are his.

  Grac. Yet, Sir, I know
How much I to your gen'rous Passion owe;
You bleed for me; and if for me you dye,
Your Loss I'll mourn with vow'd Virginity.

  Bruce. Can you be mindful of so small a Debt,
And that which you to *Beaufort* owe forget?
That will not Honour but Injustice be;
Honour with Justice always does agree,
This generous Pity which for me you show,
Is more than you to my Misfortunes owe:
These Tears, *Graciana*, which for me you shed,
O're-prize the Blood which I for your have bled:
But now I can no more ———
My Spirits faint within my VVearied Breast.

  Lovis. Sister, 'tis fit you give him leave to rest,
VVho waits?   [*Enter Servants.*
VVith Care convey him to his Bed.

  Bruce. Hold ———
Dearest *Aurelia*, I will strive to live,
If you will but endeavour not to grieve.

  Lovis. Brave Man! the wonder of this Age thou'lt prove,
For Matchless Gratitude, and gen'rous Love.
                                        [*Exeunt all but* Graciana.

  Grac. How strangely is my Soul perplext by Fate,
The Man I love, I must pretend to hate!
And with dissembled Scorn his Presence fly,
VVhose Absence is my greatest Misery!

                                        Enter

Enter Beaufort.

Beauf. Hear me, upon my Knees I beg you'll hear.
She's gone.   [*Exit* Graciana.
There was no need, false VVoman, to encrease
My Misery with hopes of Happiness.
This Scorn at first had to my Love and me
But Justice been ; now it is Cruelty.
VVas there no way his Constancy to prove.
But by your own Inconstancy in Love ?
To try another's Virtue cou'd you be,
Graciana, to your own an Enemy ?
Sure, 'tis but Passion which she thus does vent,
Blown up with Anger and with Discontent,
Because my Honour disobey'd her VVill,
And *Bruce* for love of her his Blood did spill.
I once more in her Eyes will read my Fate ;
I need no VVound to kill me if she hate.

SCENE II.

Enter Cully *drunk, with a blind Fellow led before him playing on a*
Cymbal, follow'd by a number of Boys hollowing, and
persecuting him.

Cul. Villains, Sons of unknown Fathers,
Tempt me no more.   [*The Boys bout at him, he draws his Sword.*
I will make a young Generation of Cripples,
To succeed in *Lincolns-Inn-Fields,* and *Covent-Garden.*
The barbarous breeding of these *London* Boys!   [*Frights the Boys away.*
Boy that leads the Cymbal. Whither do you intend to go, Sir ?
Cul. To see the wealthy VVidow, Mrs. *Rich.*
Boy. Where does she dwell, Sir ?
Cul. Hereabouts ; enquire, I will Serenade her
At Noon-Day.   [*Exeunt.*

Enter the Widow and her Maid Betty.
Wid. Where is this poor Frenchman, Girl ?
H'as done me good Service.
Betty. The Butler has got him down into the Cellar, Madam,
Made him drunk, and laid him to sleep among
His empty Casks.
Wid. Pray, when he wakes let him be releas'd of his Imprisonment ;
Betty, you use your Servant too severely.
                                    [*The Cymbal plays without.*
                                                    Hark,

Hark, what ridiculous Noife is that? it fets my Teeth an edge,
VVorfe than the fcraping of Trenchers.

Enter a Servant.

Serv. Madam, a rude drunken Fellow, with a Cimbal before him,
And his Sword in his hand is prefs'd into your Houfe.

Enter Cully and Cimbal: The Women fhriek.

Cull. Sirrah play me a bawdy Tune, to pleafe the VVidow:
Have at thee VVidow.

Betty. 'Tis one of *Oliver's* Knights, Madam,
Sir *Nicholas Cully*; his Mother was my Grandmother's
Dairy-Maid.

Enter Servants; they lay hands on him, and take away his Sword.

Cull. Let me go; I am not fo drunk but I can ftand
Without your help, Gentlemen.
Widow, here is Mufick; fend for a Parfon,
And we will dance *Barnaby* within this
Half hour.

Wid. I will fend for a Conftable, Sir.

Cull. Ha'ft a mind to fee me beat him? how thofe Rogues dread me!
Did not *Wheadle* tell thee upon what Conditions
I won'd condefcend to make thee my Bed-fellow,
Widow, fpeak?

Wid. This is fome drunken Miftake; away with him,
Thruft him out of door.

Enter a Servant: Clafhing of Swords and Noife without.

Serv. Help, help, for Sir *Frederick.*

Wid. What's the matter?

Serv. He's fighting, Madam, with a Company of Bayliffs,
That wou'd arreft him at the Door.

Wid. Hafte every one, and refcue him quickly.   [*Exeunt all but* Cully.

Cul. Widow, come back, I fay, VVidow;
I will not ftir one Foot after thee:
Come back, I fay, VVidow.   [*Falls down and fleeps.*

Enter Dufoy.

Dufoy Vat de diablé be de matré? here is de ver
Strange Varke in dis houfe; de Vemen dey do
Cry, ha, ha, ha; de Men dey do run, dey do
Take de Batton, de Dung-Vorké, and de Vire-Vorké;
Vat is here, van killé?   [*Looking on* Cully.

Enter Betty.

Betty. You are a trufty Servant, indeed: here you are lock'd up,
While your poor Mafter is arrefted, and drag'd away
By unmerciful Bailiffs.

Dufoy. My Matré? Jernie! Metres *Bet*, letté me go:

Begar

Begar I vil kill allé de Bogre
De Bailié, and recover my Matré. Bogre de Bailié.

Betty. So make all the haste you can,   [*She helps him out of the Tub.*

Dufoy. Morbleu ! Bogre de Bailié !
I vil go prepare to kill a tousand Bailié,
Begar : Bogre the Bailié.   [*Exit.*

                Enter the Widow *and* Servant, *severally.*

Wid. Well, what News ?

Serv. Madam, they have arrested him upon an
Execution for Two hundred Pounds, and carried
Him to a *Bayliff's* House, hard by.

Wid. If that be all, *Betty,* take my Key, and give him
The Money in Gold ; do you content the *Bayliffs,*
But let Sir *Frederick* know nothing of it ;
And then let them bring him to my House,
As their Pris'ner : Dispatch.   [*Exeunt* Betty *and* Servant.

                Enter a Foot-Boy.

Foot-B. Pray, Madam, is there not a stray Gentleman
Mis-led by Drink ?

Wid. There lies the Beast you look for ;
You had best remove him quickly,
O I shall cause him to be put into the Pound.   [*Ex.* Widow.

Foot-B. If I do not get this Fool clear off before he
Comes to himself, our Plot is quite spoil'd :
This Summer-Livery may chance to hover over
My shivering Limbs next Winter.
Yonder sits honest *Palmer,* my poor Master,
In a Coach, quaking for fear ; all that
See him in that Reverend Disguise,
Will swear he has got the Palsie.
Ho, Sir *Nich'las.*   [*Pulls him.*

Cul. I will drink three Beer-glasses to the Widow's
Health, before I go.

Foot-B. The Widow stays for you, to wait upon her
To the Exchange.

Cul. Let her go into her Bed-Chamber and meditate ;
I am not drunk enough to be seen in her Company.

Foot-B. I must carry him away upon my back : but
Since things may go ill, 'tis good to make sure
Of something : I'll examine his Pockets first :
So, for this I thank my own Ingenuity ;
In this VVay of plain Dealing, I can live without
The Help of my Master.   [*Enter a Servant.*

Pray, Sir, will you help me up with my Burden ?

                                      Serv.

Serv. I'm sure your Master has his Load already.   [*They lift him up.*
Cul. Carry me to my Widow, *Boy*: Where is my
Musique?

    Enter Sir Frederick *with the Bayliffs, who are Fidlers disguis'd, with
    their Fiddles under their Coats, at one Door, and the Widow
    at another.*

Boy. There is no Hope now;
I'll shift for my self.   [*Exit Boy.*

    Sir *Fred.* Widow, these are old Acquaintance of mine,
Bid them welcome: I was coming
To wait upon you before; but meeting
Them by the way, they press me to drink———
          [*Cully reells against* Sir Frederick.

    Cul. Sir *Frederick*! Widow, bid him welcome;
He is a very good Friend of mine, and as mad a Fellow as my self.
Kiss, kiss the Widow, Man; she has a plump
Under-Lip, and kisses smartly.

    Sir *Fred.* What's here? *Cully* drunk, transform'd into a Gallant,
And acquainted with the Spring and Proportion
Of the Widow's Lips!

    Cul. I, I am drunk, Sir; am I not, Widow?
I scorn to be soberer than your self, I will drink with you,
Swear with you, break Windows with you,
And so forth.

    Sir *Fred.* Widow, Is this your Champion?
    Wid. You have no Exception against him, I hope;
He has challenged you at your own VVeapons.

    Cul. Widow, Sir *Frederick* shall be one of our *Bride-Men*;
I will have none but such mad Fellows at our VVedding;
But before I marry thee I will consider upon it.   [*He sits down and sleeps.*

    Sir *Fred.* Pray, VVidow, how long have you been acquainted
With this Mirrour of Knighthood?

    Wid. Long enough you hear, Sir, to treat of Marriage.
    Sir *Fred.* VVhat, you intend me for a Reserve then?
You will have two *Strings* to your *Bow*, VVidow;
I perceive your Cunning; and Faith, I think, I shall
Do you the heartier Service, if thou employ'st me by the bye.

    Wid. You are an excellent Gallant indeed; shake off
These lousie Companions; Come, carry your Mistress
To the Park, and treat her at the Mulberry-Garden,
This glorious Evening.

    Sir *Fred.* Widow, I am a Man of Business,
That Ceremony's to be perform'd by idle Fellows.

    Wid. VVhat won'd you give to such a Friend as shou'd dispatch

                           This

This bufinefs now, and make you one of thofe idle Fellows.

Sir Fred. Faith, pick and chufe; I carry all my wealth about Me; do it, and I am all at thy fervice, VVidow.

Wid. Well, I have done it, Sir; you are at liberty, And a leg now will fatisfie me.

Sir Fred. Good Faith, thou art too reafonable, dear Widow; Modefty will wrong thee.

Wid. Are you fatisfi'd?

Fidl. Yes, Madam.

Enter Dufoy, *with a Helmet on his head, and a great Sword in his hand.*

Dufoy. Vare are de bougre de Baylié? Tetibleu, bougre Rogue.   *[He falls upon the Fidlers.*

Fidl. Help, help, Sir *Frederick*, murder, murder! alas, Sir, we Are not Bayliffs: you may fee we are men of an honefter Vocation.   *[They fhew their Inftruments.*

Sir Fred. Hold, hold, thou mighty Man at Arms.

Dufoy. Morbleu, de Fidler! and is my Matré at liberty? play Me de Trichaté, or de Jegg Englifhé, quicklie, Or I vill make you all dance Vidout your Fiddle; quiké.

Wid. I am over-reach'd, I perceive.   *[Dufoy dances a Jig.*

Sir Fred. Kind Widow, thank thee for this releafe. *[Shakes his Pockets.* Laugh, Widow; ha, ha, ha: where is your counterplot, VVidow? Ha, ha, ha. Laugh at her, *Dufoy.* Come, Be not fo melancholy; we'll to the Park: I care not if I fpend a piece or two upon thee in Tarts and Cheefcakes. Pifh, VVidow, why fo much out of humour? 'Tis no fhame to love fuch a likely Young Fellow.

Wid. I cou'd almoft find in my heart to punifh my felf, To afflict thee, and marry that drunken Sott I never Saw before.

Sir Fred. How came he hither?

Wid. Enquire elfewhere; I will not anfwer thee one Queftion; nor let thee fee me out of a Mask any more This Fortnight.

Sir Fred. Go, go into thy Clofet, look over thy old Receipts, And talk wantonly now and then with thy Chambermaid; I fhall not trouble thee much till this is fpent;   *[Shakes his Pockets.* And by that time thy foolifh Vow will be near over.

Wid. I want patience to endure this infolence.

Is my Charity rewarded thus ?

Sir *Fred.* Pious Widow, call you this Charity ? 'twill get
Thee little hereafter ; thou muſt anſwer for ev'ry ſin
It occaſions : Here is Wine and Women
In abundance.   [*Shakes his Pockets.*

Wid. Avoid my Houſe, and never more come near me.

Sir *Fred.* But hark you, hark you, VVidow, do you think
This can laſt always ?

Wid. Ungrateful Man !   [*Exit Widow.*

Sir *Fred.* She's gone ; impatience for theſe two hours
Poſſeſs her, and then I ſhall be pretty well
Reveng'd.

Duſoy. Begar, Matré, have you not de ver faithful
Serviteur ? you do never take notice of my merit.

Sir *Fred.* *Duſoy,* thou art a Man of Courage, and haſt done
Bravely ; I will caſt off this Suit a VVeek ſooner than
I intended, to reward thy ſervice.

Duſoy. Begar I have ſeveral time given you ver
Dangerous teſtimonié of my affection.

                 Enter a Servant, and takes up Cully *in his arms.*

Sir *Fred.* VVhither do you carry him ?

Serv. Sir, there is an old Gentleman below in a Coach,
Very like my Lord *Bevil,*
VVho, hearing what a condition Sir *Nich'las* was in,
Deſired me to bring him to him in my arms.

Cul. Let me go, where is the VVidow ?

Sir *Fred.* VVhat VVidow ?

Cul. Miſtreſs *Rich* ; ſhe is to be
My VVife.

Sir *Fred.* But do you hear, Sir *Nich'las* ? how long have you
Courted this VVidow ?

Cul. Mr. *Wheadle* can tell you : trouble me not with idle
Queſtions, Sir *Frederick.*
You ſhall be welcome at any time ; ſhe loves Men
That will roar, and drink, and Serenade her.

Sir *Fred.* This is ſome ſtrange miſtake ; ſure *Wheadle* intending
To chouſe him, has ſhew'd him ſome counterfeit VVidow ;
And he being drunk, has been miſguided to the true
VVidows Houſe. The Fellow in the Coach may
Diſcover all ; I will ſtep and ſee who it is :
Hold him here, *Duſoy,* till I return : Gentlemen,
Come you with me.   [*Exit Sir* Frederick *and Fidler.*

Cul. VVhere is my Miſtreſs ?

Duſoy. Vat Metres ?

                                                    Cul.

Cul. The Widow.

Dufoy. She be de Metres of my Matré.

Cul. You lye, Sirrah.

Dufoy. Begar you be de Jackanape to tellé
Me I do lyea.

Cul. You are a French Rafcal, and I will blow
Your nofe without a Handkerchief.   [*He pulls* Dufoy *by the nofe.*

Dufoy. Helpé, helpé me; Morbleu; I vil beat you vid my fifté
And my footé, tellé you aské me de pardon; take
Dat and daté; aské me de pardon.
                              [Cully *falls down, and* Dufoy *beats him.*

Cul. I ask you pardon, Sirrah?

Dufoy. Sirrah? Tettibleu.   [*Offers to ftrike.*

       Enter Sir Frederick *and Fidlers, leading in* Palmer *trembling.*

Sir Fred. Hold, hold, Dufoy.

Dufoy. Begar he do merite to be beaté; he fwaré he vil
Marré youré Metres.

Palm. I befeech you, Sir *Frederick.*

Cul. My Lord *Bevil!*

Sir Fred. So, he takes him for my Lord *Bevil;*
Now the Plot will out.
'Tis fit this Rafcal fhou'd be cheated;
But thefe Rogues will deal too
Unmercifully with him: I'll take compaffion upon
Him, and ufe him more favourably my felf.

Cul. My Lord, where is the mad Wench your Sifter?
                              [*Sir* Frederick *pulls off* Palmer's *difguife.*

Sir Fred. Look you, Sir *Nich'las,* where is my Lord *Bevil*
Now?

Cul. My merry Country-man, Mr. *Palmer!* I thought you had
Been in *Buckinghamfhire.*   [*Sings.*

          And he took her by the Apron,
          To bring her to his beck.

Never a Catch now, my merry Country-man?
Sir *Frederick,* I owe this Gentleman a thoufand Pounds.

Sir Fred. How fo?

Cul. He won it of me at Dice, *Wheadle* went my halfs;
And we have given him a Judgment for it.

Sir Fred. This was the roguery you had been about the other
Night, when I met you in difguife, *Palmer;*
You'l never leave your cheating and your robbing,
How many Robberies do I know

Of your committing?

Palm. The truth is, Sir, you know enough to hang me;
But you are a worthy Gentleman, and a lover of Ingenuity.

Sir Fred. This will not pass:
Produce the Judgment.

Palm. Alas, Sir! Mr. *Wheadle* has it.

Sir. Fred. Produce it, or —— Fetch the Constable, Boy.

Palm. Sir *Frederick*, be merciful to a sorrowful Rascal:
Here is a Copy of the Judgment, as it is entred.

Sir Fred. Who is this counterfeit VVidow? confess.

Palm. Truly 'twas *Wheadle*'s contrivance; a Pox on him:
Never any good comes on't when men are so unconscionable
In their Dealings.

Cul. VVhat am I cheated, Sir *Frederick*? Sirrah,
I will have you hang'd.

Sir Fred. Speak, who is this Widow?

Palm. 'Tis *Grace*, Sir, *Wheadle*'s Mistress, whom he has plac'd
In my Lady *Dawbwel*'s House: I am but a poor Instrument,
Abus'd by that Rascal.

Sir Fred. You see, Sir *Nich'las*, what Villains these are; they have
Cheated you of a Thousand Pounds, and would have married
You to a VVench, had I not discover'd their Villany.

Cul. I am beholding to you, Sir *Frederick*, they are Rogues,
Villanous Rogues: But where's the VVidow?

Sir Fred. VVhy, you saw the true Widow here a little while
Ago.

Cul. The truth is, methoughts she was something comlier
Than my Mistress: But will not this VVidow.
Marry me?

Sir Fred. She is my Mistress.

Cul. I will have none of her then.

Sir Fred. VVell, I have discover'd this Cheat, kept you from
Marrying a VVench, and will save you a thousand Pounds too.
Now, if you have a mind to marry, what think you of my Sister?
She is a plain brown Girl, and has a good Portion;
But not out Twenty Thousand Pound: This Offer proves
I have a perfect Kindness for you.

Cul. I have heard she is a very fine Gentlewoman;
I will marry her forthwith, and be your Brother-in-Law.

Sir Fred. Come then, I'll carry you where
You may see her, and ask her Consent.
Palmer, you must go along with us,
And by the way assign this Judgment over to me.
Do you guard him, Gentlemen.   [*To the Fidlers.*

                                                      Sir

Sir *Fred.* Come, Sir *Nich'las.*

Cul. How came I hither?

Sir *Fred.* You will be satisfied in that hereafter.

Palm. What cursed accident was this? what
Mischievous Stars have the managing
Of my Fortune? Here's a turn with all my heart
Like an after-game at *Irish*!

Dufoy. Alon marché, Shentelmen sheté;
Marché: You make de mouthé of
De honest Shentelmen: begar you vil make de
Wry mouthé ven you be hangé.   [*Exeunt.*

SCENE III.

Scene, A Garden.

Enter Graciana *and* Leticia *severally*; Leticia *with a Nosegay
in her Hand.*

Grac. *Leticia*, what hast thou been doing here?

Let. Cropping the beauty of the youthful year.

Grac. How innocently dost thou spend thy hours,
Selecting from the crowd the choicest Flowers!
Where is thy Mistress?

Let. Madam, she's with the wounded Colonel.

Grac. Come then into this Arbour, Girl, and there
With thy sweet Voice refresh my wearied Soul. [*They walk into an Arbour.*

SONG.

Ladies, though to your Conq'ring Eyes   [*Let. sing.*
    Love owes his chiefest Victories,
And borrows those bright Arms from you
With which he does the World subdue.
    Yet you your selves are not above
    The Empire nor the Griefs of Love.

Then wrack not Lovers with disdain,
Lest Love on you revenge their Pain;
You are not free because y're fair;
The Boy did not his Mother spare.
    Beauty's but an offensive dart;
    It is no Armour for the heart.

Grac.

Grac. Dear Girl, thou art my little Confident ;
I oft to thee have breath'd my difcontent ;
And thy fweet Voice as oft has eas'd my care :
But now thy breath is like infectious Air.

                     Enter Beaufort.

It feeds the fecret caufe of my difeafe,
And does enrage what it did ufe t'appeafe.

    Beauf. ftarting. Hark, that was *Graciana*'s Voice.

    Grac. Oh *Beaufort* !

    Beauf. She calls on me, and does advance this way :
I will conceal my felf within this Bower : fho may
The fecret caufes of my grief betray.

           Beaufort *goes into an Arbour,* and Graciana *and* Leticia
                          upon the Stage.

    Grac. Too rigidly my Honour I purfue ;
Sure fomething from me to my Love is due :
Within th fe private fhades for him I'll mourn,
Whom I in publick am oblig'd to fcorn.

    Let. Why fhou'd you, Madam, thus indulge your grief ?
Love never yet in forrow found relief :
Thefe Sighs, like Northern Winds to th' early Spring,
Deftruction to your blooming Beauty bring.

    Grac. Leticia, peace ; my Beauty I defpife :
Wou'd you have me preferve thefe fatal Eyes ?

    Let. Had you lefs beauteous been, y'ad known lefs care :
Ladies are happieft moderately fair :
But now fhou'd you your Beauty wafte, which way
Cou'd you the debt it has contracted pay ?

    Grac. Beaufort, didft thou but know I weep for thee
Thou would'ft not blame my fcorn, but pity me.

    Let. VVhen Honour firft made you your Love decline,
You from the Centre drew a crooked line :
You were to *Beaufort* too fevere, I fear,
Left to your Love you partial might appear.

    Grac. I did what I in honour ought to do :
I yet to *Beaufort* and my love am true :
And if his Rival live, I'll be his Bride,
Joy fhall unite whom Grief does now divide :
But if for love of me brave *Bruce* does die,
I am contracted to his Memory.
Oh, *Beaufort* !

    Beauf. Oh, *Graciana !* here am I
(By what I've heard) fix'd in an ecftafie.

Grac. We are furpriz'd; unlucky accident!
Frefh Sorrow's added to my difcontent.

[*Exeunt* Graciana *and* Leticia *leifurely.*
Beaufort *enters.*

Beauf. Graciana, ftay, you can no more contend,
Since Fortune joins with Love to be my Friend;
There is no fear of *Bruce* his death; the wound
By abler Chir'gions is not mortal found.
She will not ftay.
My Joys, like Waters fwell'd into a flood,
Bear down whate're their ufual ftreams withftood.   [*Exit* Beaufort.

SCENE IV.

Scene, My Lady *Dawbwel*'s Houfe.

Enter Wheadle *and* Grace.

Whead. I wonder we have yet no tidings of our Knight,
Nor *Palmer,* ——
Fortune ftill croffes the induftrious, Girl
VVhen we recover him you muft begin
To lie at a little opener ward;
'Tis dangerous keeping the Fool too long at bay,
Left fome old VVood-man drop in by chance,
And difcover thou art but a rafcal Deer.
I have counterfeited half a dozen Mortgages,
A dozen Bonds, and two Scriveners to vouch all;
That will fatisfie him in thy Eftate:
He has fent into the Country for his
VVritings:
But fee, here he comes.

Enter Sir Nicholas.

Sir *Nich'las,* I muft chide you, indeed I muft;
You neglect your duty here: Nay, Madam, never
Blufh; Faith I'll reveal all. Y'are the happieft,
The luckieft Man ——

Enter Sir Frederick.

W'are betray'd; Death, what makes him here?
Sir *Frederick,* your humble Servant; y'are come   [*To Sir* Frederick.
In the luckieft time for mirth; will you but lend
Me your Ear? do not you fee Sir *Nich'las* and *Grace*
Yonder? look, look.

Sir *Fred.* Yes.

Whead. I am perfwading him to keep her; fhe's a pretty

Deferving

Deferving Girl ; 'faith let us draw off a while,
And laugh among our felves, for fear of fpoiling
The poor Wenches market ; let us, let us.

   Sir Fred. VVith all my heart.

        Bayliffs meet VVheadle *at the door, and Arreft him.*

   Bayliffs. VVe arreft you, Sir.

   Whead. Arreft me? Sir *Frederick*, Sir *Nicholas.*

   Sir Fred. VVe are not provided for a Refcue at prefent, Sir.

   Whead. At whofe Suit?

   Bayliffs. At Sir *Frederick Frollick*'s?

   Whead. Sir *Frederick Frollick*'s? I owe him never a farthing.

   Sir Fred. Y'are miftaken, Sir ; you owe me a thoufand pounds:
Look you, do you know Mr. *Palmer*'s hand?
He has affign'd fuch a fmall debt over to me.

        Enter Palmer *and* Jenny.

   Whead. How was I bewitch'd to truft fuch a Villain!
Oh Rogue, Dog, Coward, *Palmer.*

   Palm. Oh thou unconfcionable *Wheadle* ; a thoufand pounds
Was too fmall a bubble!

   Sir Fred. Away with him, away with him.

   Whead. Nay, Sir *Frederick*, 'tis punifhment enough to fall
From my expectation :
Do not ruine a young man.

   Grac. I befeech you, Sir.

   Sir Fred. Thou haft mov'd me, *Grace* ;
Do not tremble, Chuck ; I love thy profeffion too well
To harm thee.
Look you, Sir, what think you of a rich Widow? [*Proffering him the Whore.*
Was there no Lady to abufe, *Wheadle*, but my Miftrefs?
No man to bubble but your Friend and Patron, Sir *Nich'las* ?
But let this pafs ; Sir *Nich'las* is fatisfi'd ; take *Grace*
Here, marry her, we are all fatisfi'd:
She's a pretty deferving Girl, and a Fortune now
In earneft ; I'll give her a thoufand pounds.

   Whead. Pray, Sir, do but confider ——

   Sir Fred. No confideration ; difpatch, or
To Limbo.

   Whead. Was there ever fuch a Dilemma? I fhall rot in Prifon.
Come hither, *Grace* ; I did but make bold, like a young Heir,
With his Eftate, before it come into his hands:
Little did I think, *Grace*, that this Pafty,   [*Stroaking her Belly.*
When we firft cut it up, fhould have been preferv'd
For my Wedding-Feaft.

   Sir Nich. You are the happieft, the luckieft man, Mr. *Wheadle.*

                               Palm.

Palm. Much Joy, Mr. *Wheadle*, with your rich Widow.

Whead. Sir *Frederick*, Shall that Rogue, *Palmer*, laugh at me?

Sir *Fred.* No, no; *Jenny*, Come hither; I'll make thee amends,
As well as thy Miſtreſs, for the Injury I did thee
Th' other Night:
Here's a Husband for thee too:
Mr. *Palmer*, where are you?

Palm. Alas, Sir *Frederick*, I am not able
To maintain her!

Sir *Fred.* She ſhall maintain you, Sir,
Do not you underſtand the Myſtery of *Stiponie*,
Jenny?

Maid. I know how to make *Democuana*, Sir.

Sir *Fred.* Thou art richly endow'd, i'faith: Here, here, *Palmer*;
No ſhall I, ſhall I: This or that, which
You deſerve better.

Palm. This is but a ſhort Reprieve; the Gallows will
Be my Deſtiny.

Sir *Fred.* Sir *Nicholas*, now we muſt haſte to a better
Solemnity; My Siſter expects us.
Gentlemen, meet us at the *Roſe*; I'll beſtow a Wedding
Dinner upon you, and there releaſe your Judgment,
Mr. *Wheadle*.
Bayliffs, wait upon them thither.

Sir *Nich.* I wiſh you much Joy with your fair Brides,
Gentlemen.

Whead. A Pox on your Aſſignment, *Palmer*.

Palm. A Pox on your rich Widow, *Wheadle*:
Come, Spouſe, Come.   [*Exeunt.*

SCENE V.

Scene, *The Lord* Bevil's *Houſe*.

Enter Lord Bevil, Bruce *led in,* Lovis, Beaufort, Graciana
and Aurelia.

Bruce. Graciana, I have loſt my Claim to you,
And now my Heart's become *Aurelia's* due;
She all this while, within her tender Breſt,
The Flame of *Love* has carefully ſuppreſt,
Courting for me, and ſtriving to deſtroy
Her own Contentment to advance my Joy.

Aurel. I did no more than Honour preſs'd me to;
I wiſh I'd woo'd ſucceſsfully for you.

K   *Bruce*

Bruce. You fo excel in Honour and in Love,
You both my Shame and Admiration move.
Aurelia, Here, accept that Life from me,
Which Heav'n fo kindly has preferv'd for thee.
My Lord, I hope you will my Choice allow,   [*To L.* Bevil.
And with your Approbation feal our Vow.

    Bevil. In gen'rous Minds this to the World will prove
That Gratitude has Pow'r to conquer Love.
It were, brave Man, Impiety in me
Not to approve that which the Heav'ns decree.

    Bruce. Graciana, on my gen'rous Rival you
Muft now beftow what to his Merit's due.

    Grac. Since you recovering, *Bruce,* your Claim decline,
To him with Honour I my Heart refign.

    Beauf. Such Honour and fuch Love, as you have fhown,
Are not in the Records of Virtue fhown.
My Lord, you muft affift us here once more ;   [*To L.* Bevil.
The God of *Love* does your Confent implore.

    Bev. May *Love* in you ftill feed your *mutual Fire.*   [*Joyning their Hands.*

    Beauf. And may that Flame but with our Breaths expire.

    Lovis. My Lord, our Quarrel now is at an End ;
You are not *Bruce*'s Rival, but his Friend.

    Beauf. In this brave ftrife your Friendfhip foar'd above
The active Flames of our afpiring *Love.*

    Bruce. Dear Friend, thy Merits Fame cannot exprefs.

    Lovis. They are rewarded in your Happinefs.

    Bruce. Come all into my Arms before I reft ;
Let's breathe our Joys into each others Breaft :
Thus Mariners rejoyce when Winds decreafe,
And falling Waves feem wearied into Peace.

    Enter Sir Frederick *and* Dufoy *at one Door* , *and the* Widow
        and Betty *at another.*

    Sir *Fred.* Hafte, *Dufoy,* perform what I commanded
You.

    Dufoy. I vil be ver quick begar ; I am more den half de
Mercurié.

    Sir *Fred.* Ho, Widow, the Noife of thefe Nuptials brought
You hither; I perceive your Mouth waters.

    Wid. Were I in a longing Condition, I fhould be apt
Enough to put my felf upon you, Sir.

    Sir *Fred.* Nay, I know th'art fpiteful, and wou'dft
Fain marry me in Revenge; but fo long as I have
Thefe Guardian Angels about me, I defie thee,

And all thy Charms: Do skillful Faulkners thus
Reward their Hawks before they fly the Quarry?

   Wid. When your Gorge is empty, you'll come
To the Lure again.

   Sir Fred. After I have had a little more Experience
Of the Vanity of this World, in a melancholy humour
I may be carless of my self.

   Wid. And marry some diſtreſſed Lady, that has
Had no leſs experience of that Vanity.

   Sir Fred. Widow, I profeſs the contrary; I would not have the
Sin to anſwer for, of debauching any from ſuch
Worthy Principles: Let me ſee, if I ſhould be
Good natur'd now, and conſent to give thee a Title
To thy own Wealth again, you wou'd be ſtubborn,
And not eſteem the Favour, Widow.

   Wid. Is it poſſible you can have thoughts of Gratitude?
Do you imagine me ſo Fooliſh as your ſelf,
VVho often venture all at play, to recover one inconſiderable
Parcel?

   Sir Fred. I told you how 'twould be, VVidow,
Leſs Providence attend thee, elſe I ſhall do no good upon thee:
Farewel

   Wid. Stay, Sir; let us ſhake hands at parting.

   Sir Fred. Nay if thou once art acquainted with my Conſtitution,
Thou'lt never let me go; Widow, here,
Examine, examine.   [*Holding out his hand.*

   Bevil. Siſter, I long have known your Inclinations;
Give me leave to ſerve you. Sir *Frderick*, here,
Take her, and may you make each other happy.

   Wid. Now I have receiv'd you into my Family,
I hope you will let my Maids go quietly about
Their buſineſs, Sir?

   Sir Fred. Upon Condition there be no twits of
The Good Man departed; no Preſcription pleaded
For evil Cuſtoms on the wedding Night.
Widow, what old doings will be anon!
I have coupled no leſs than a Pair-Royal my ſelf.
This day, my Lord, I hope you'll excuſe the Liberty
I have taken to ſend for them; the ſight will much
Encreaſe your mirth this Joyful Day.

   L. Bev. I ſhould have blam'd you, Sir, if you had
Reſtrain'd your Humour here.
Theſe muſt needs be pleaſant Matches that are of his
Making.

            Ente

Enter Dufoy.

Sir Fred. What, are they come?

Dufoy. Dey be all at the Dooré, begar; every Man vid his
Pret Metres, Brid, Whore.
Entré, Jentlemen, vid your Lady, entré vid your
Great Fortuné: Ha, ha, ha.

Enter Sir Nicholas *and his Bride,* Wheadle *and his Bride,* Palmer
and his Bride.

Sir Nich. Brother, do you fee how fneakingly *Wheadle* looks
Yonder with his rich Widow?

Wid Brother! is this Fellow your Brother?

Sir Nich. Ay, that I am.

Sir Fred. No, no, Sir *Nicholas.*

Sir Nicholas, Did not I marry your Sifter, Sir?

Sir Fred. Fie, fie, Sir *Nich'las;* I thought y'ad been
A modefter Man.

Sir Nich. Is my Wife no kin to you, Sir?

Sir Fred. Not your Wife; but your Son and Heir may,
If it prove fo. * Joy be with thee old Acquaintance.   [* *To* Lucy
Widow, refolving to lead a virtuous Life,
And keep houfe altogether with thee,
I have difpos'd of my own Houfhold-ftuff,
My dear Mrs. *Lucy,* to this Gentleman.

Whead and Palm. We wifh you Joy with your fair Bride,
Sir *Nich'las.*

Sir Nich. I will go and complain, and have you all clap'd up
For a Plot immediately.

Sir Fred. Hold, hold, Sir *Nich'las,* there are certain
Catch-poles without: you cannot fcape,
Without y'ave a thoufand Pounds in your
Pocket: Carry her into the Country, come;
Your Neighbours Wives will vifit her, and vow
She's a vertuous well-bred Lady:
And, give her her due, 'faith fhe was a very
Honeft Wench to me, and I believe will make a very
Honeft Wife to you.

Sir Nich. If I difcover this I am loft; I fhall be ridiculous
Even to our own Party.

Sir Fred. You are in the right: Come, take her,
Make much of her, fhe fhall fave you
A Thoufand Pounds.

Sir Nich. Well, *Lucy,* if thou canft but deceive my
Old Mother, and my Neighbours in the Country,
I fhall bear my Fortune patiently.

Sir Fred. I'll warrant you, Sir, Women so skill'd in Vice
Can dissemble Virtue.

Dufoy. Fy, fy, maké de much of your Lady, Shentlemen;
Begar you vil find them ver civil.

Sir Fred. Dufoy, I had almost forgot thee.

Dufoy. Begar my merit is ver seldom in your
Memorié.

Sir Fred. Now I will reward thy Services; here,
Enjoy thy Mistress.

Dufoy. Ver vel, begar; you will give me two tree oldé
Gowné vor all my diligence.

Betty. Marry come up! Is that a despicable Portion
For your greasie Pantaloons?

Dufoy. Peace, peace, Metres *Bet*; ve vil be ver good
Friend upon Occasion; but ve vil no marrié:
Dat be ver much better, begar.

Sir Fred. Did you bring the Bailiffs with you?

Dufoy. Dey be vidout: Begar, Shentlemen, you have bin
Made ver sad; and you shall now be made ver mer
Vid de Fidler.

Whead. Ha! cozen'd with Fidlers for Bailiffs!
I durst have sworn false Dice might as soon have
Pass'd upon me.

Sir Fred. Bid them strike up; we will have a Dance,
Widow, to divert these melancholy Gentlemen.   [*They Dance.*

L. Bevil. Sir *Frederick*, You shall command my House this Day;
                                                    [*After the Dance.*

Make all those welcome that are pleas'd to stay.

Sir Fred. Sir *Nicholas*, and Mr. *Wheadle*, I release you both
Of your Judgement, and will give it under
My hand at any Time.
VVidow, for all these bloody Preparations,
There will be no great Massacre of Maiden-Heads
Among us here.
Anon I will make you all laugh with the Occasion
Of these VVeddings.

On what small Accidents depends our Fate,
VVhilst Chance, not Prudence, makes us Fortunate.

EPILOGUE,

EPILOGUE.

Spoke by the Widow.

SIR Frederick, *now I am reveng'd on you,*
  For all your Frollick Wit, y'are couzen'd too :
I have made over all my Wealth to these
Honest Gentlemen ; they are my Trustees.
Yet, Gentlemen, if you are pleas'd you may
Supply his Wants, and not your Trust betray.

Spoke by *Wheadle.*

Poor Wheadle *hopes h'as gi'n you all content ;*
Here he protests 'tis that he only meant :
If y'are displeas'd we're all cross-bit to day,
And he has wheadl'd us that writ the Play.

THE

THE
EPILOGUE.

Like Pris'ners, conscious of th' offended Law,
  When Juries after th' Evidence withdraw;
So waits our Authour, between Hope and Fear,
Until he does your doubtful Verdict hear.
Men are more civil than in former Days;
Few now, in Publick, hiss or rail at Plays;
He bid me therefore mind your Looks with Care,
And told me I should read your Sentence there;
But I, unsklli'd in Faces, cannot guess
By this first View what is the Play's Success;
  Nor shall I ease the Authour of his Fear,
  Till twice or thrice, at least, I've seen you here.

FINIS.

CPSIA information can be obtained at www.ICGtesting.com
Printed in the USA
LVOW03s2121250915

455753LV00015B/347/P